TIME
FOR KIDS

BIG
BOOK OF
HOW

TIME FOR KIDS
Managing Editor, TIME FOR KIDS: Nellie Gonzalez Cutler
Editor, Time Learning Ventures: Jonathan Rosenbloom

Book Packager: R studio T, New York
Art Direction/Design: Raúl Rodriguez and Rebecca Tachna
Writer: Curtis Slepian
Illustrator: Felipe Galindo
Photo Researcher: Elizabeth Vezzulla
Special Thanks to: Harry Chamberlain, Anne Jewell, Zane Martin,
Donna Moxley Scarborough, Neil Soderstrom, Turkey Hill Dairy

Time HOME ENTERTAINMENT

TIME HOME ENTERTAINMENT
Publisher: Richard Fraiman
General Manager: Steven Sandonato
Executive Director, Marketing Services: Carol Pittard
Executive Director, Retail & Special Sales: Tom Mifsud
Executive Director, New Product Development: Peter Harper
Director, Bookazine Development & Marketing: Laura Adam
Publishing Director, Brand Marketing: Joy Butts
Assistant General Counsel: Helen Wan
Design & Prepress Manager: Anne-Michelle Gallero
Book Production Manager: Susan Chodakiewicz
Associate Marketing Manager: Jonathan White
Associate Prepress Manager: Alex Voznesenskiy

Special Thanks to: Christine Austin, Jeremy Biloon, Alex Borinstein, Glenn
Buonocore, Malati Chavali, Jim Childs, Rose Cirrincione, Jacqueline Fitzgerald,
Christine Font, Lauren Hall, Carrie Hertan, Suzanne Janso, Raphael Joa, Mona Li,
Robert Marasco, Kimberly Marshall, Amy Migliaccio, Nina Mistry, Richard Prue, Dave
Rozzelle, Myles Ringel, Ilene Schreider, Sasha Shapiro, Soren Shapiro, Adriana Tierno,
Time Imaging, Vanessa Wu

For information on TIME For Kids magazine for the classroom or home, go to
WWW.TFKCLASSROOM.COM or call 1-800-777-8600.

For subscriptions to Sports Illustrated Kids, go to www.sikids.com or call 1-800-889-6007.

Published by TIME For Kids Books
Time Inc.
1271 Avenue of the Americas
New York, New York 10020

ISBN 10: 1-60320-907-7
ISBN 13: 978-1-60320-907-6

"TIME For Kids" is a trademark of Time Inc.

We welcome your comments and suggestions about TIME For Kids Books.
Please write to us at:
TIME For Kids Books
Attention: Book Editors
PO Box 11016
Des Moines, IA 50336-1016

If you would like to order any of our hardcover Collector's Edition books, please call us
at 1-800-327-6388. (Monday through Friday, 7:00 a.m.– 8:00 p.m. or Saturday,
7:00 a.m.– 6:00 p.m. Central Time).

1 QGT 11

Contents

How to Use This Book 5

Chapter 1: Animals

How Do Elephants Communicate? 6
How Do Sharks Find Prey? 8
How Do Chameleons Change Colors? 10
How Does a Snake Inject Its Venom? 12
How Did the Dinosaurs Die Out? 14
How Do Animals See at Night? 16
How Does a Spider Spin Its Web? 18
How Do Honeybees Make Hives? 20
How Do Beavers Build Dams? 22
How to Make Blubber 24
How to Mark Your Territory..........................26

Chapter 2: Be Prepared

How to Stay Safe in a Hurricane 28
How to Stay Safe in a Storm.............................30
How to Stay Safe During an Earthquake..........32
How to Stay Safe in a Fire...............................34
How to Stay Safe During a Tornado...................36
How Does a Search Dog Find a Missing Person?.38
How to Make a Compass................................ 40
How to Make a Survival Kit 42

Chapter 3: Sports

How Does an Arena Change an Ice Rink
into a Basketball Court?........................44
How Are Baseball Bats Made?................46
How Does Hockey Equipment Keep
Players Safe?........................ 48

How Do You Do a Skateboard
Trick Called an Ollie?........................50
How Do You Do the Snowboarding Trick
Called Butter?........................52
How Do Ice Skaters Spin So Fast?......................54
How Can You Stay Upright on a Surfboard?....56
How Can You Prevent Sports Injuries? 58
How Do Bicycle Gears Make You Go Faster? ... 60
How Does Motion Capture Technology
Help Athletes? 62
How to Make a High-Bounce Ball 64
How to Find the Sweet Spot on a Bat 66

Chapter 4: Buildings

How Were the Egyptian Pyramids Built?.......... 68
How Was Mount Rushmore Built? 70
How Does the Panama Canal Work? 72
How Was a Bridge Built Across the
Colorado River? 74
How to Build a Spaghetti Bridge 76
How to Build a Pyramid 78

Chapter 5: Science

How Do Scientists Uncover and Remove
Fossils from a Dig? 80
How Are Oil Spills Cleaned Up?........................ 82
How Are Birds Cleaned Up After an Oil Spill? ... 84
How Do Roller Coasters Go Up and
Down? 86
How Do Optical Illusions Trick Our Eyes? 88
How Is a Fireworks Show Staged? 90

How Does an Iceberg Form? 92

How to Make a Rain Forest 94

How to Grow Crystals 96

Chapter 6: Transportation

How Do Submarines Work? 98

How Does a Hybrid Car Work? 100

How Are Tunnels Dug? 102

How Does a Maglev Train Work? 104

How to Make a Baking-Soda Boat 106

How to Make a Paper Airplane 108

Chapter 7: Home Tech

How Does a Microwave Oven Cook Food? .. 110

How Does a Lock Work? 112

How Does a Toilet Flush Away Waste? 114

How Does a Zipper Zip? 116

How Does a Refrigerator Keep Food Cold?... 118

How Can a Virus Make Your Computer Sick?... 120

How Does Wi-Fi Connect to the Internet?........ 122

How to Make Your Own Camera 124

How to Make a Periscope............................. 126

Chapter 8: Food

How Does Popcorn Pop? 128

How Does Bread Rise? 130

How Is Chocolate Made? 132

How Is Ice Cream Made? 134

How Do Chili Peppers Make Your
Mouth Burn?................................... 136

How to Make Ice Cream 138

How to Make Pizza 140

Chapter 9: Space

How Can We Protect Earth from Big
Space Rocks? 142

How Will the Juno Probe Uncover
Jupiter's Secrets? 144

How Do Astronauts Train? 146

How Does the Sun Stay Hot? 148

How Do We Know If There's Another Earth
Out There? 150

How to Build a Planetarium 152

How to Launch a Rocket 154

Chapter 10: The Human Body

How Does the Stomach Digest Food? 156

How Do We Cry? 158

How Do Medicines Work? 160

How Do Eyeglasses Help Us See Better? 162

How Does the Body Fight Germs? 164

How Does Loud Music Hurt Your Hearing? ... 166

How to Make a Stethoscope....................... 168

How to Find Your Dominant Eye 170

Chapter 11: Going Green

How Are Computers and Other Electronics
Recycled? 172

How Can You Make Your House Greener? ... 174

How Do Wind Turbines Make Electricity? 176

How to Make Your Own Landfill 178

How to Make Recycled Paper 180

Glossary 182

Index 186

Photo Credits.. 192

HOW to Use This Book

This book has all the questions...and the answers. If you've ever wondered how the dinosaurs died out, how a toilet works, or how to perform a skateboard trick called an ollie, you'll find out in these pages. The book is divided into 11 chapters that cover topics ranging from sports and science to food and animals. At the end of the chapters, you'll find some hands-on activities and experiments. The book is also full of unsual facts that'll have you saying, "How about that!" A glossary at the end defines some of the terms used in the book.

Introduction: This will give you a brief background about the topic to help you understand both the question and the answer.

Factoids: Read these to learn some amazing facts and trivia about the subject.

Information boxes: Brief articles and lists enrich your understanding of the topic.

Diagram and photos: Visuals and captions combine to provide a clear answer to the question.

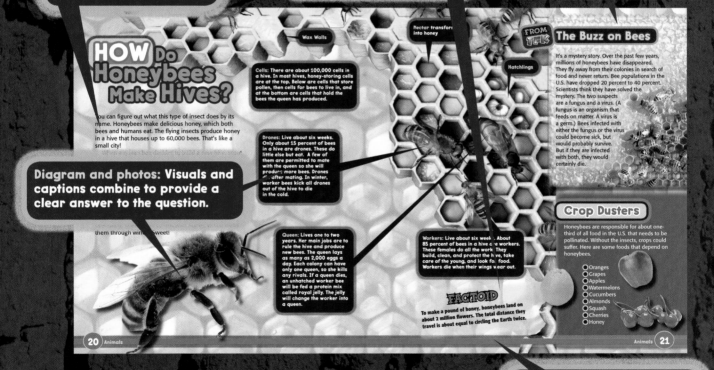

HOW Do Honeybees Make Hives?

You can figure out what this type of insect does by its name. Honeybees make delicious honey, which both bees and humans eat. The flying insects produce honey in a hive that houses up to 60,000 bees. That's like a small city!

them through winter. Sweet!

Wax Walls

Nectar transform into honey

Hatchlings

Cells: There are about 100,000 cells in a hive. In most hives, honey-storing cells are at the top. Below are cells that store pollen, then cells for bees to live in, and at the bottom are cells that hold the bees the queen has produced.

Drones: Live about six weeks. Only about 15 percent of bees in a hive are drones. These do little else but eat. A few of them are permitted to mate with the queen so she will produce more bees. Drones die after mating. In winter, worker bees kick all drones out of the hive to die in the cold.

Queen: Lives one to two years. Her main jobs are to rule the hive and produce new bees. The queen lays as many as 2,000 eggs a day. Each colony can have only one queen, so she kills any rivals. If a queen dies, an unhatched worker bee will be fed a protein mix called royal jelly. The jelly will change the worker into a queen.

Workers: Live about six weeks. About 85 percent of bees in a hive are workers. These females do all the work. They build, clean, and protect the hive, take care of the young, and look for food. Workers die when their wings wear out.

FACTOID
To make a pound of honey, honeybees land on about 2 million flowers. The total distance they travel is about equal to circling the Earth twice.

FROM TFK

The Buzz on Bees

It's a mystery story. Over the past few years, millions of honeybees have disappeared. They fly away from their colonies in search of food and never return. Bee populations in the U.S. have dropped 20 percent to 40 percent. Scientists think they have solved the mystery. The two suspects are a fungus and a virus. (A fungus is an organism that feeds on matter. A virus is a germ.) Bees infected with either the fungus or the virus could become sick, but would probably survive. But if they are infected with both, they would certainly die.

Crop Dusters

Honeybees are responsible for about one-third of all food in the U.S. that needs to be pollinated. Without the insects, crops could suffer. Here are some foods that depend on honeybees.

- Oranges
- Grapes
- Apples
- Watermelons
- Cucumbers
- Almonds
- Squash
- Cherries
- Honey

20 Animals

Animals 21

The experiments and activities in this book require adult supervision. Time Home Entertainment Inc., TIME for Kids, and R Studio T disclaim all responsibility and liability for any damage or injuries caused or sustained while performing any of these experiments or activities.

Color border: Different color borders let you quickly see what chapter you're in.

HOW Do Elephants Communicate?

Elephants don't just stand out in a crowd. They like to stand in crowds. The world's largest land mammals, elephants are very social. They enjoy hanging out in a herd. Elephants can be very chatty with plenty to say to each other.

An elephant uses just about every part of its body to send and receive messages—from trunk to tail. One way elephants communicate is through sound. Another way is through sight and movement. An elephant can flap its ears or bend its head to say anything from "I'm in a good mood" to "I'm Number 1 in this group!" Elephants also share their feelings through touch, using their bodies and trunks. Even the odors an elephant gives off, combined with a strong sense of smell, help them communicate with each other.

An elephant can learn a lot by using its trunk to smell odors produced by another elephant's urine, breath, dung, and scent glands. These scents are messages about an elephant's health and emotions.

A sac between the ear and eye gives off a liquid that looks like tears. The liquid runs when an elephant is excited by a fight or when family members return. The odor of the liquid can communicate that the elephant is ready to mate.

The first living things appeared on Earth about 3 billion years ago. Since then, animal species—from sponges to elephants— have developed fantastic features that help them survive.

As a way of saying hello, elephants of different groups will touch each other with their trunks as they pass. Males and females will entwine their trunks when they're thinking about mating.

An elephant can produce many sounds, from soft groans to screams. Each call has a meaning. Elephants know the individual sounds of hundreds of elephants. Low-frequency calls travel as far as five miles. These growls help them communicate with herds miles away.

When threatened, an elephant will raise its head and spread out its ears to look even bigger. Its message: I'm ready to fight. It pulls back its ears when it wants to communicate that it's backing down.

A Change of Tune

FROM TFK

Blue Whale

Elephants aren't the only jumbo animals to communicate using loud sounds. Blue whales are the largest animals ever to have lived on Earth. The massive mammals make big noises. Their long, low songs carry across vast ocean distances. Male blue whales use the songs to communicate with other blue whales. Researchers have found that the sound the whales make has gotten lower over the years. Low-pitched sounds don't travel as far in the ocean as high-pitched sounds.

Scientists think whales have switched to a lower pitch because the songs don't have to reach as far as they once did. In the early 1930s, blue whales were almost hunted to extinction so they had to look farther away to find other whales. Higher-pitched songs helped the animals locate each other.

In recent years, the whale population has bounced back. So high-pitched songs may no longer be necessary.

HOW Do Sharks Find Prey?

Sharks are swift and silent killers. Many large sharks, such as the great white, have big appetites. They will track down and eat seals, sea lions, and other marine animals. They'll even swallow garbage floating around in the ocean, such as license plates and metal cans. Although most sharks don't like people on their menu, the big fish will take a bite out of humans.

Sharks in one form or another have been swimming in Earth's oceans for more than 400 million years. One ancient shark was 52 feet long and had teeth the size of a person's hand. Today's sharks are smaller, but they remain at the top of the food chain in the sea. A close look at their bodies shows why they are such hardy survivors. From nose to tail, they're packed with sensing equipment that helps them locate their prey.

A shark can smell even a tiny drop of blood in the water from hundreds of yards away. It can detect one drop of blood in one million drops of water. That's the same as smelling a teaspoon of juice in a swimming pool.

Small openings in the shark's skin called electroreceptors detect tiny electrical fields created by the heartbeat and muscle movements of other fish. This lets sharks hunt for prey that might be hiding under sand.

A shark can see in dim light because its eyes are about 10 times more sensitive to light than human eyes. Some sharks have a membrane that covers and protects the eyes when it attacks prey.

FACTOID

Sharks are hungry even before they are born. When they are inside the mother, sharks develop teeth. Sometimes one unborn shark will eat its unborn brothers and sisters.

Tiny holes on top of the head lead to very sensitive ears. A shark can pick up the sound of a struggling fish more than 800 feet away.

A row of vibration-sensitive hair cells runs along the shark's sides. They allow a shark to sense the faintest motion of a fish from about 3 to 10 feet away.

Shark Attack!

Sharks prefer eating other marine animals to eating people. Still, the number of shark attacks has been up in recent years. Researchers think one reason is that there are more people swimming, boogie-boarding, and surfing than ever before. Volusia County, Florida, holds the national record for shark attacks because it has a long coastline and its beaches are packed with bathers. Sharks may think a human foot is a flounder, then spit out human flesh after the first bite.

Actually, humans are a bigger threat to sharks than sharks are to people. Fishing nets catch and drown about 100 million sharks each year.

FACTOID

Sharks can live for a long time. The average lifespan is about 25 years, but some have been known to live to 100.

HOW Do Chameleons Change Color?

Chameleons can change their colors in seconds from brown to green to red to blue. Experts believe light, temperature, and mood affect the lizard's color. A chameleon might turn from brown to green to reflect sunlight and stay cool. Or it might become darker to absorb the sun's heat. An angry chameleon can turn dark red or yellow to warn other chameleons to back off.

The secret to this color explosion is skin deep. Under a chameleon's skin is a layer made up of red or yellow pigment (color) cells. Another layer reflects white and blue light. Yet another layer has particles called melanin, which can make colors darker.

Nerve cells direct color cells to get bigger or smaller or cause melanin to spread throughout other layers. If a chameleon is angry, the yellow cells might expand. Various pigments blend to produce different colors. For example, if the yellow cells expand and more blue light reflects upwards, the chameleon turns green. (Mixing yellow and blue creates green.)

Eyes: Move independently of each other, so each eye can look at different objects at the same time.

Long tongue: Can be one and a half times its body length.

To change color, a chameleon makes its color cells get **larger** or smaller. It can also make its skin darker by letting a chemical called melanin rise to the upper cell layers.

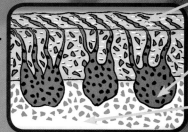

Red and yellow color cells

Melanin layer

Blue and white cell layers

Fingers and toes: Are able to grip branches.

Skin: Is green or brown when the chameleon is resting. This helps it blend into the background. Pigments under the skin change the lizard's color, depending on temperature, sunlight, and mood.

Body: Is narrow and shaped like a leaf, making it easy to blend in on trees, where chameleons hang out.

Tail: Is prehensile, meaning it can curl and wrap around branches.

Color Guard

Here are some other animals that protect themselves by changing their colors.

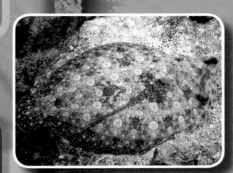

Flounder

As it swims along the bottom of the sea, the fish can change its color and patterns in seconds to blend in with the ocean floor. It can make itself look like almost anything, from sand to pebbles. A flounder can even make itself transparent, so no enemy can see it.

Panamanian Tortoise Beetle

For birds, this beetle is a tasty treat. To avoid being eaten, the beetle can change its color from gold to red. The beetle's outer shell has many layers. When patches between layers are wet, the shell looks gold. When the patches dry out, the shell becomes clear, and a layer of red pigment becomes visible. Predators leave the now-red beetle alone because it looks like a poisonous insect.

Goldenrod Crab Spider

This arachnid hangs out on either white or yellow flowers, waiting for a tasty meal to come along. If the spider is on a yellow flower, it squeezes a liquid yellow pigment into its outer cell layer. If it sits on a white flower, it gets rid of yellow liquid so only white cells show.

HOW Does a Snake Inject Its Venom?

Most snakes are not dangerous. Some are even helpful. Snakes kill rodents and rabbits, which can destroy crops. And a snake's venom, or poison it gives off, may one day help treat human diseases. Only a third of the nearly 3,000 known snake species around the world are venomous, or poisonous. In the United States, only four snake species are dangerous to people. They are the rattlesnake, cottonmouth moccasin, copperhead, and coral snake.

All snakes eat meat by swallowing prey whole. Some, like the boa constrictor and reticulated python, wrap themselves around a victim and crush it to death before eating. Other snakes swallow living prey. Then there are the snakes that kill prey with a venomous bite. Even the most poisonous snake doesn't want to attack humans because we are too big to swallow. But if surprised or frightened, a snake will strike out at a person. So be very careful if you see one in the wild.

The venom gland is an organ that produces venom, a poisonous liquid.

Venom from the venom gland passes through a duct into the fangs.

Some venomous snakes jab their fangs into the victim. The fangs are hollow so poison can squirt into the prey. In other snakes, poison flows along grooves in the fangs and into the bitten prey.

DID YOU KNOW?

To avoid being bitten by a snake:
- Never handle a snake unless you're with an expert.
- When hiking, avoid tall grass. Stay on the hiking path.
- Don't climb any rock, or use caution if you do, to avoid surprising a snake.
- Wear heavy hiking or walking shoes—don't go barefoot or wear sandals.

Different types of snakes make different venoms. There are three main types: one causes the victim to stop breathing. Another destroys heart muscle. The third makes blood vessels burst.

A snake milker is a person who collects snake venom. The venom is used to help make a cure for snake bites. The milker massages the snake's venom glands. This forces the snake to spit its venom into a jar.

Keep Back!

Snakes aren't the only animals that can deliver a knockout punch packed with poison. Here are some of the most toxic animals in the world.

Poison Arrow Frog

Don't pick up this little amphibian, native to Central and South American rain forests. Its skin contains a toxic chemical that sickens or kills any animal that touches or eats it. The amount of toxin that can fit on the head of a pin will kill a large mammal—or an unlucky person.

Stonefish

If you swim off Australia's coast, keep away from any fish that look like rocks or pieces of coral. A stonefish's powerful toxin, stored in its 13 spines, is deadly to the touch.

Box Jellyfish

Found in ocean waters around Asia and Australia, this sea creature should be avoided at all costs. It carries its poisons in its tentacles and its stingers.

HOW Did the Dinosaurs Die Out?

The dinosaurs never saw it coming. The first dinosaurs appeared on Earth about 230 million years ago. Dinosaurs (the name means "terrible lizards") ruled the planet for nearly 165 million years. Then, about 65 million years ago, they all disappeared. Along with the dinos, about 50 percent of all the planet's plants and animals were wiped out in a mass extinction. An extinction is when an entire species dies out. What caused this huge wipeout? Some scientists once thought dinosaurs got too big to survive. Others believed dino eggs were eaten by mammals. Now, scientists have come up with other possible reasons.

Blowing Their Tops

Before the dinos died out, huge volcanic eruptions took place in Western India. They covered half of modern-day India with a layer of volcanic rock one mile thick. Clouds of ash and dust could have blotted out the sun, lowering the planet's temperatures. Volcanic gases may have produced acid rain, which hurt plant and sea life. These disasters could have led to mass extinctions.

Bad Bugs

As the planet's temperature rose 65 million years ago, it became a perfect breeding ground for germs and insects. The insects could have spread new diseases that dinosaurs and other animals couldn't fight off.

The Big Crash

A comet or asteroid about six miles across may have slammed into the Yucatan, in Southern Mexico, 65 million years ago. The blast sent clouds of dust into Earth's atmosphere. Trillions of tons of burning ash from the blast may also have set fire to forests, creating clouds of smoke. The dust and smoke blocked the sunlight for years and so temperatures dropped. The result: global cooling that did away with the dinos.

Here Today . . .

Some scientists think a mass extinction may be going on right now. They estimate that 30,000 species disappear each year. That's three species an hour. By the end of this century, half of today's species of plants and animals could disappear. The main cause for this: humans.

A species is endangered when it is in immediate danger of becoming extinct. A threatened species is likely to become endangered in the future. Once a species is extinct, it will never come back. Here is just a handful of animal species that are endangered or threatened.

- Gray bat
- Louisiana black bear
- Siberian tiger
- California condor
- Whooping crane
- Rhinoceros
- Black footed ferret
- Southern sea otter
- Marine turtles
- Giant panda
- Coho salmon
- Sperm whale

Sea This

Scientists believe that Earth's oceans were once much higher than they are today. Then, millions of years ago, the continents rose and sea levels dropped. Many once-wet areas became cool and dry. During that period, for example, North America was divided by a sea called the Interior Seaway. As the ocean levels lowered, the Seaway drained. Not only did many sea animals die, but the dry land could no longer produce the food that dinosaurs needed to survive. This may have led to their dying out.

HOW Do Animals See at Night?

For most people, night is the time to catch some zzzz's. But many animals start their day at sundown. Animals that sleep during the day and are active at night are called nocturnal. For them, night time is the right time.

For a lot of nocturnal critters, finding food in the dark depends on great eyesight. Their eyes are specially adapted to let them see in dim light. Unlike these creatures, it takes humans a while to adjust to darkness. In poor light, humans can only see shades of black and white and not much detail. That's why we keep stubbing our toes at night! But nocturnal animals adjust instantly. The vision of some animals is so sharp, they can pick out small objects in total darkness.

The giant peepers of the tarsier, a tiny primate from Southeast Asia, let it see at night.

The Nocturnal Eye

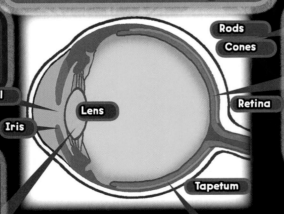

The pupils open wider than those of humans at night. This lets nocturnal animals take in more light.

Pupil

Lens

Iris

Rods

Cones

Retina

Tapetum

A nocturnal animal doesn't have many cones, or color-sensitive cells, in its retina. Instead, the retina is packed with rods, which are cells that detect black and white. These cells work in dim light and can sense motion.

Some animals with eyeballs that can't move have rounded lenses. Rounded lenses let the animal focus light coming in from any angle.

The tapetum (tah-*pee*-tum) is a thin membrane behind the retina, which contains cells sensitive to light. When light passes through the retina, the tapetum reflects it back like a mirror. This gives the retina a double-dose of light, making it easier to see in darkness.

In the Dark!

Animals have all kinds of special adaptations that let them hunt—and avoid hunters—in dim light and in total darkness.

Owl

It has great night vision thanks to a very wide retina, an iris that opens up to twice the width of a hawk's, and a lens that works like a telescope. It can focus on a mouse more than the length of a football field away on a dark night.

Pit Viper

Tiny pits on each side of this snake's face sense the warmth of an animal. The pits allow the snake to sense the size and shape of an object. The pit viper can tell if it is a possible meal or not worth hunting.

Bats

Bats send out a high-pitched sound that bounces off objects, including tasty insects. The bats use the echoes to "see" what's around them.

Monitor Lizard

A monitor's eyesight isn't great, but its tongue makes up for it. As the tongue flicks out, it tastes scents in the air. The tongue places the scent on the roof of its mouth, where special cells tell the lizard what's out there to eat—or hide from.

HOW Does a Spider Spin Its Web?

Itsy bitsy spiders—and some that aren't so itsy bitsy—live everywhere on Earth, except for the polar regions. They crawl around in dry deserts, on mountains, below ground, in oceans—and possibly in some corners of your home.

Most spiders are web masters. A gland in their abdomen produces silk. The silk is pushed through a body part called a spinneret and comes out as a thread. Some spiders spin silk webs that look like big white sheets. Some webs look like tiny drops stretched across plants or grass. One of the most common webs is the orb web, which is shown in the photo. This is the kind you see on Halloween or in a spooky haunted house in scary movies. A spider waits at the center of the orb web for a tasty insect to land. This makes the web vibrate. The spider knows from the vibration whether or not it is food. If the spider is lucky, dinner is served!

Making an Orb Web

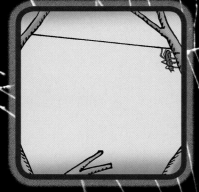  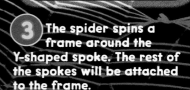

1 The spider finds a good spot, such as a tree branch, and makes a strand. The dangling strand sticks to another branch. The spider attaches the other end of the strand to the branch it's standing on. Then it crosses back and forth over that strand, strengthening it with more strands.

2 The spider makes a loose strand connecting the two ends of the first strand. Next it drops down a strand at the middle of the loop to form a Y shape. These three strands are the first spokes of the web.

3 The spider spins a frame around the Y-shaped spoke. The rest of the spokes will be attached to the frame.

A Real Spider-Man

FROM TFK

Steven Kutcher knows spiders. He is an entomologist, a scientist who studies insects. People in Hollywood call him a bug wrangler. For more than 20 years, Kutcher has been rounding up bugs and helping them get roles in movies and TV. He worked on the first three *Spider-Man* movies, as well as many others in which insects played a supporting role.

During "auditions," Kutcher doesn't look for insects that can act. He looks for bugs that can get the job done. For *Spider-Man*, for instance, Kutcher studied what the spider would have to do—spin a web, climb a wall. Then he determined which type of spider would perform the task best.

Kutcher hopes that insect-filled movies will help turn bug-fearing folks into fans.

The spider's silk comes out of the spinneret.

4 The spider makes more spokes. Each spoke is close so the spider can walk on one while making another. Spokes also must be close enough so the spider can walk across them when the web is complete. These threads are not sticky.

5 When the spokes are finished, the spider makes a few circular threads in the center of the web to make it strong. Then it spins a spiral of non-sticky thread from the center of the web to the edge of the frame. This helps the spider construct the rest of the web.

6 The spider spins many more spiral strands using sticky threads. When finished, the spider will remove the non-sticky spiral. Total time for building the web: 30 minutes. Some spiders build a new web every day, while others just repair any damage.

HOW Do Honeybees Make Hives?

Wax Walls

Cells: There are about 100,000 cells in a hive. In most hives, honey-storing cells are at the top. Below are cells that store pollen, then cells for bees to live in, and at the bottom are cells that hold the bees the queen has produced.

You can figure out what this type of insect does by its name. Honeybees make delicious honey, which both bees and humans eat. The flying insects produce honey in a hive that houses up to 60,000 bees. That's like a small city!

When a queen bee decides to build a new hive, scout bees may travel miles to find a tree hollow or other good spot. The scouts lead a swarm of bees to this new location. Honey from the old hive is used to start the new one. Bees chew on honey to turn it into beeswax. The wax is shaped into thousands of six-sided cells. A few layers of cells are called a honeycomb. Workers build combs starting at the top of the hive and work downward. They stick the combs to the roof and walls, making sure there are passageways between the combs. Eventually, bees fill the combs with honey, which feeds them through winter. Sweet!

Drones: Live about six weeks. Only about 15 percent of bees in a hive are drones. These do little else but eat. A few of them are permitted to mate with the queen so she will produce more bees. Drones die after mating. In winter, worker bees kick all drones out of the hive to die in the cold.

Queen: Lives one to two years. Her main jobs are to rule the hive and produce new bees. The queen lays as many as 2,000 eggs a day. Each colony can have only one queen, so she kills any rivals. If a queen dies, an unhatched worker bee will be fed a protein mix called royal jelly. The jelly will change the worker into a queen.

Nectar transformed into honey

Hatchlings

The Buzz on Bees

It's a mystery story. Over the past few years, millions of honeybees have disappeared. They fly away from their colonies in search of food and never return. Bee populations in the U.S. have dropped 20 percent to 40 percent. Scientists think they have solved the mystery. The two suspects are a fungus and a virus. (A fungus is an organism that feeds on matter. A virus is a germ.) Bees infected with either the fungus or the virus could become sick, but would probably survive. But if they are infected with both, they would certainly die.

Workers: Live about six weeks. About 85 percent of bees in a hive are workers. These females do all the work. They build, clean, and protect the hive, take care of the young, and look for food. Workers die when their wings wear out.

FACTOID

To make a pound of honey, honeybees land on about 2 million flowers. The total distance they travel is about equal to circling the Earth twice.

Crop Dusters

Honeybees are responsible for about one-third of all food in the U.S. that needs to be pollinated. Without the insects, crops could suffer. Here are some foods that depend on honeybees.

- Oranges
- Grapes
- Apples
- Watermelons
- Cucumbers
- Almonds
- Squash
- Cherries
- Honey

HOW Do Beavers Build Dams?

The beaver is the master builder of the animal world. These furry architects can build dams as long as one-half mile (that's twice the length of Hoover Dam!) and strong enough to hold the weight of a human. They also construct well-ventilated homes with underwater entrances.

To make themselves safe from predators, such as foxes, beavers often build a dam that creates a pond or a large lake. They'll then build a lodge, or house, in the lake. These lodges are like little islands that keep the beaver safe from the outside world. Beavers often live in the same lodge for years. So these North American rodents spend much of their time repairing their home. Even in winter beavers stay active, swimming in the pond, looking for food, working on their house. No wonder people use the expression "busy as a beaver."

Tunnels: Beavers build tunnels to enter and exit the lodge, or house. The tunnels are built under the water to keep out enemies. A second tunnel allows a quick escape, just in case some animal manages to enter.

Dam: Beavers begin the dam at the narrow part of a stream. They cut down nearby trees, remove branches, and drag logs to the bottom of the stream. Beavers add rocks, grass, leaves, broken branches, and mud to the logs to make the dam watertight. The job is done when the running water is blocked. A lake or pond forms behind the dam.

FACTOID

A beaver can use its teeth to cut down a six-inch wide aspen tree in 20 minutes.

Lodge: Beavers build a lodge in the lake. These dome-shaped homes are usually about 10 feet high and 20 feet wide. Beavers plant sticks in the bottom mud of the pond, then add bark, rocks, mud and anything else they can find to build up the lodge.

Vent hole: A small hole at the top of the lodge allows hot air to escape and lets the air inside move around.

Chambers: The tunnel enters a chamber, or room, where beavers store and eat food. Beavers also sleep and take care of their young, called kits, in chambers. Each lodge is home to up to 18 family members.

Animal Architects

Beavers aren't the only animals that build things. These are some top critter construction workers.

Termites
These tiny insects are the skyscraper builders of the animal world. They can create nests up to 30 feet high and 40 feet in diameter.

Bowerbird
The male bowerbird makes a bower, or shelter, on a forest floor using objects such as twigs, leaves, flowers, and moss. It decorates the inside with whatever it can find, including feathers, pebbles, shells, coins, aluminum foil, and spoons.

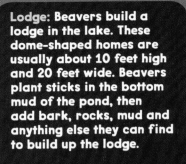

Caddisfly
The larva, or young form, of this insect builds and carries around a small structure called a case. The portable house is built of spun silk, plus bits of twigs, sand, shells, and human trash.

HOW to Make Blubber

Brrrrr! That's what most people shout when they jump into cold water. Humans can't swim very long in very chilly water without a wet suit. But marine mammals, like polar bears and walruses, have no problem diving into icy seas. How come? One word: blubber.

Blubber is a thick layer of fat that insulates animals. It keeps their body heat from escaping into the cold water. There is blubber in many sea creatures, including whales, dolphins, porpoises, seals, manatees, and dugongs. The thickness of the blubber ranges from a few inches in dolphins and polar bears to a foot in some whales. Blubber is also a source of energy. When there's no food around, marine mammals can live off their fatty layers. Humans have a layer of fat too, but it doesn't do much insulating. Try this experiment to see how blubber can keep you warm.

What You Need

- Vegetable shortening, such as Crisco
- 2 ziplock sandwich bags
- A bowl of ice water with ice cubes

What to Do

1 Put vegetable shortening into one ziplock bag until it's one-third filled.

2 Turn the other ziplock bag inside out. Place it inside the bag filled with shortening, and spread out the shortening in an even layer. The shortening should be trapped between the two bags like a layer of blubber.

FACTOIDS

- Blubber can make up to 50 percent of the body weight of some marine mammals. A blue whale has up to 50 tons of blubber.

- Blubber is a better insulator than fur for marine animals. Fur can get squashed and lose its insulating powers.

3 Put your hand into the inside-out bag. Zip closed each bag as much as possible to make them waterproof. If you can't zip them, tape the opening to make the bags as airtight as possible.

4 Put your bare hand into the ice water to feel how cold it is. Then put your blubber mitten into the ice water. Does the water seem colder with the mitten hand or with the bare hand? Now imagine that the layer of shortening in the blubber is a few inches thick. How warm would it keep your hand?

FACTOID

Some types of whales can go six months without eating. They live off the blubber they saved up in the previous six months.

Keeping Warm

Blubber is just one way animals keep warm when the temperature drops. They have plenty of other cool ways to deal with the cold.

Anti-Freeze The temperatures in Arctic and Antarctic waters would freeze solid the bodily fluids of most fish. But not the Arctic cod and other fish that swim in these waters. They have a kind of anti-freeze inside them. A special gene makes proteins that keep the blood of these fish from freezing.

Fur Sure Many Arctic animals have thick fur to stay warm. Besides its blubber, the polar bear has two layers of hair that keep it toasty. An outer layer of long, oily hair repels water. An inner layer of shorter hairs traps heat near the polar bear's skin.

Winter Pause Cold-blooded animals, such as snakes, frogs, and lizards, shut off their body systems during winter. They can live half alive, half dead, for weeks at a time.

Shape Shifter The Arctic fox is rounder than foxes that live in warmer areas. A round, plump shape holds in more heat than a longer shape. Arctic animals also tend to have shorter ears, tails, and legs, so less heat escapes.

Dig Deep Small mammals, like mice and voles, dig little underground nests, called burrows, and doze through the cold days. Bears and some other larger mammals hibernate, or sleep, through winter. They save energy during their winter-long snooze.

HOW to Mark Your Territory

"Keep Out!" Humans mark off their property with signs, fences, doors, and walls. Some animals also mark their property, or territory. (A territory is the area in which an animal nests, hunts for food, and often mates.) They do it to warn other animals of the same species to keep out. But animals have their own way of hanging up a "No Trespassing!" sign.

Some critters might snarl or hiss or sing or roar. Tigers and coyotes leave scratch marks in trees to warn off rivals. Many mammals use odor to mark the border of their territory. They may spray urine against trees or on the ground. Or they might rub up against objects to leave scents produced by scent glands. Do you think you could detect the border of a territory by smell?

FACTOID

A male panda bear uses scent to mark its territory. The scent also shows how big and powerful the bear is: It stands on its hands and marks as high up on a tree as it can.

What You Need
- A friend
- Two clean, empty spray bottles
- White vinegar
- Food extract, such as mint, peppermint, orange, vanilla, or lemon

What to Do

1 Fill both spray bottles about half-way with water.

2 Pour vinegar into one spray bottle until it is about two-thirds full of liquid.

3 Put drops of the food extract into the other spray bottle. Add the drops until the smell is strong.

4 Close the tops of both spray bottles. Give one to a friend.

5 Go outside and each of you choose a territory. Close your eyes and have your friend spray the boundary of his or her territory on the ground. The boundary should be made with straight lines. Have your friend close his or her eyes while you mark your territory by spraying straight lines on the ground.

6 Detect each other's territory. Walk around the ground until you sniff your friend's smelly boundary lines. You might have to get on your knees to catch the aroma. Try to show the boundary with rocks, leaves, or pieces of paper. Marking a small territory isn't too difficult. But imagine what it's like to mark and guard a territory every few days that is miles long.

Pet Power Play

Cats and dogs are cute pets, but they sometimes behave like animals in the wild. Like wolves and tigers, dogs and cats mark territory. They will stake a claim in your home, on objects you own, even on you.

A cat has scent glands on its cheeks and the sides of its body. It will rub against things, including its owner, to leave its scent. The scent tells other cats, "This belongs to me. Get lost!" Cats also leave their scents when they scratch things. The scent comes from the pads of their paws. A cat also marks its territory by raising its tail to spray urine as a marker.

Dogs mark their territory and show that they are the "top dog" mostly by urinating. A dog will squirt against places and objects to show who's the boss. The chemicals in the urine let other dogs know who made the mark and how long ago it was left. Dogs also have a much louder way to mark their territory: barking.

FACTOID

It's s sticky situation. The okapi, an African animal, marks its territory with scent glands on its feet. The glands give off a tar-like substance wherever it walks.

HOW to Stay Safe in a Hurricane

Hurricanes are huge storms that can cause destruction to large areas. They can last more than a week, can have wind speeds of 160 miles per hour or more, and can be as wide as 500 miles. Hurricanes only form over water. Because of that, states along the Gulf of Mexico and the east coast of the U.S. are often the hardest hit.

Hurricane winds can toss objects around and shatter glass. But the most dangerous part of a hurricane is the storm surge. A storm's powerful winds push ocean water over the shore, causing floods. Storm surges account for most of a hurricane's damage. But if your family is prepared for a hurricane, you will be safe while you sit out the storm.

FACTOID

The deadliest hurricane in U.S. history struck Galveston, Texas, in 1900, before there were instruments that could track a hurricane's path and warn people. The storm flooded the island-city, killing 8,000 people.

Before a Hurricane Strikes

- Make plans to keep your home and property safe. Windows should be covered by built-in storm panels or boarded up with plywood. Tape won't keep windows from breaking.

- Listen to the radio or TV for information.

- Close the storm shutters. Tie down outdoor objects or bring them indoors.

- Turn off gas and electricity if told to by officials.

- Don't use the phone except for emergencies.

- Be sure there is a supply of food to eat and water for drinking and flushing toilets.

- Leave your home if ordered to by local authorities. Follow their instructions.

- If you live in a building with many stories, go to the lowest level—hurricane winds are stronger at higher levels.

- If you live on a coast, or in an area near water and can't escape the storm:

  • Stay indoors during the hurricane and away from windows and glass doors.

  • Close all doors inside and outside your home.

  • Stay in a small inner room, closet, or hallway on the lowest level.

  • Lie on the floor under a table or another strong object.

Tornadoes, earthquakes, and other natural disasters don't strike often. And you may never have to escape a fire. Still, it's always important to know what to do in case of an emergency.

After the Storm

- Don't return to a home that was damaged by floodwater before local officials declare the area safe.
- Use a phone only to report life-threatening emergencies.
- Stay off the streets. There can be electrical wires on the ground, as well as weakened walls, bridges, roads, and sidewalks.
- Don't enter a home without an adult. They should make sure there are no loose power lines, gas leaks, or damage to the structure of the building.
- Enter the home carefully and check for damage. Be careful of loose boards and slippery floors.
- Never eat food touched by floodwater.

FROM TFK

Hurricane Season

From June to November, storms churn over the Atlantic Ocean. Sometimes they become hurricanes that hit the islands of the Caribbean and the coast of the U.S. Take a look at how wet weather, wind, and warm ocean waters whip up these powerful storms.

1. Born in West Africa
When hot, dry air from the Sahara Desert meets cooler air from the Sahel region, small storms form.

2. Across the Atlantic
Some storms remain small. But a few gather warm ocean moisture, speeding up as they travel west. When bands of these thunderstorms form a swirling pattern, the new system is called a tropical depression.

3. The Storm Strengthens
Winds spin around the "eye" at the storm's center. It is either a tropical storm or a hurricane, depending on the wind speed.

4. After the Storm
Hurricanes weaken over land. Some storms never hit land. Instead, they turn northeast and die out over the Atlantic Ocean.

Other winds affect the storm
Sometimes winds near a hurricane blow in the same direction. They can help the hurricane gain strength. Winds blowing in different directions or at different speeds can tear the storm apart.

NORTH AMERICA
Atlantic Ocean
EUROPE
4
3 *Hurricane*
2 *Storm system*
AFRICA
Sahara
Sahel
1
Pacific Ocean
Nearby winds
SOUTH AMERICA

HOW to Stay Safe in a Storm

Lightning is nature's fireworks. This awesome force can heat the air to a temperature of 18,000°F to 60,000°F. That's hotter than the surface of the sun. The heat makes the air expand and vibrate until it produces a booming thunderclap. Every thunderstorm contains lightning, but lightning can hit you even if the storm is 10 miles away and the sky above you is cloudless. That's what's known as a "bolt from the blue."

A lightning strike can cause a lot of damage. A single bolt holds up to one billion volts of electricity. Like fireworks, lightning should be viewed from a distance—and a safe place.

Before Thunder and Lightning Arrive

- If you see lightning and hear thunder within 30 seconds, it means the storm is within six miles of you. Seek shelter.

- If you see lightning in the upper clouds during a thunderstorm, be careful. This kind of lightning can strike many miles away from the storm. Try to get indoors.

If You're Outside

- Immediately get inside a building or hard-top automobile. If lightning strikes a car, the electricity will go harmlessly into the ground. Rubber tires and rubber-soled shoes won't protect you from lightning.

- Don't stand near trees or other tall objects in an open area.

- Avoid open fields, the top of a hill, or the beach. If you're in a boat, get to land right away and seek shelter.

- Don't go into a shed or other small structure in open areas like an athletic field or park.

- Don't stand next to or touch anything metal, such as a car, bicycle, or lamppost.

- If you are swimming, get out of the water immediately. Water is a good conductor of electricity.

- In an open area or anywhere else, if your hair stands up, it could mean that conditions are right for a lightning strike. Scrunch down into a ball so you make as little contact as possible with the ground. Don't lie flat on the ground.

If You're Inside

- Do not shower, bathe, or use a landline phone during a thunderstorm. A cell phone is safe to use.

- Unplug all electrical appliances, including TVs and computers. Turn off air conditioners. Lightning can cause power surges, which can damage equipment.

- Don't touch anything that conducts electricity and leads to the outside, such as window frames and pipes.

- Stay indoors for at least 30 minutes after you hear the last thunderclap.

Building a Bolt

Ever get shocked by a spark of static electricity in the winter? That spark is a mini version of a lightning bolt. Static electricity takes place when an object packed with a charge of electrons suddenly gets rid of the charge all at once. The same thing happens in a cloud during a storm.

Inside the cloud, currents of air rise and fall. An updraft carries droplets of water at the bottom of the cloud to a freezing region 35,000 to 75,000 feet high. At the same time, downdrafts send ice and hail from the top of the cloud to the bottom. When the water droplets and icy particles bump each other, electrons get knocked off the rising particles and collect on the falling particles. Soon, the bottom area of the cloud has a negative charge and the top has a positive charge.

Positive and negative charges attract each other. The electric field between the top and bottom of the cloud builds up until a giant spark of electricity—a lightning bolt—shoots from one part of the cloud to the other. Lightning can also strike between two clouds. Sometimes, the electrical charge will shoot from the cloud to the ground. But almost four-fifths of all lightning strikes take place inside the clouds.

HOW to Stay Safe During an Earthquake

Shake, rattle, and roll. That's what things do during an earthquake. When Earth's crust shifts, the ground trembles and shudders. Sometimes the shaking isn't very noticeable—hanging lights can sway or a vase might tumble. But when a strong earthquake hits, houses can come apart and highways crumble.

Unlike hurricanes and many other natural disasters, earthquakes hit without warning and can come in waves. You can't know for sure if another, even stronger earthquake will strike again. If you live in an area that has earthquakes, you probably have had drills at school so you'll know how to stay safe. But here are some reminders for you to share with your family.

Prepare for an Earthquake

- Have the entire family learn what to do during an earthquake. Practice what you have learned. For some tips, go to earthquake.usgs.gov.
- Identify the safest places in each room to take cover. During family drills, practice going to those areas.
- Write down the addresses and phone numbers for where your family members are during the day, such as schools and businesses. All the members of your family should carry this list.

During an Earthquake

If you are indoors:

- Drop to the floor, take cover by getting under a strong desk or other piece of furniture, and hold on until the shaking stops. If there isn't a desk or table, cover your head with your arms and crouch down in an inside corner of the building.

- Keep away from glass, windows, outside doors and walls, and anything that can fall, such as bookshelves and hanging lights.

- If you are in bed when a quake hits, stay there. Put a pillow over your head for extra safety. If you are under something that could topple on you, move to a safer place.

- Only stand in a doorway if it is close to you and you are sure it can support the weight of the building.

- Don't leave until the shaking stops and you are certain it is safe to go outside.

- Never use the elevator during an earthquake.

If you are outdoors:

- Stay outdoors, and move away from buildings, streetlights, and electrical wires.

- Stay in the open until there is no more shaking.

About 500,000 earthquakes are detected around the world each year. About 100,000 are noticed by people and only 100 cause any damage.

An earthquake hit Haiti in 2010, killing about 200,000 people. It also caused billions of dollars of damage.

Shake but Don't Break

In 1995, a powerful earthquake struck the city of Kobe, in Japan. The shaking destroyed wooden houses and collapsed steel and concrete buildings made in the 1960s. But newer buildings designed to survive earthquakes didn't fall apart.

Architects, engineers, and scientists have made lots of progress in building structures that will stay standing during a quake. Buildings often collapse when they sway back and forth during an earthquake. But earthquake-proof buildings don't sit directly on the ground. Instead, they float on ball bearings, springs, or padded cylinders. During a quake, the buildings move with it, swaying a few feet from side to side. This keeps the structure standing.

Engineers have developed sensors to make these buildings even safer. The sensors detect shaking and "tell" the building how to move. This cuts down on how much the structure shakes.

New technology will continue to protect buildings and the people in them during a quake.

Structures that are not built to withstand earthquakes may crumble during a powerful quake. This building is in Concepcion, Chile, a city that was hit by a quake in 2010.

After an Earthquake

- When the shaking stops, make sure everyone is okay.
- Adults should check the home for areas made unsafe by the earthquake.

HOW to Stay Safe in a Fire

Do you know what to do if you smell smoke in your home? Most people don't. That's the point of Fire Prevention Week, held every year in early October. During the week, firefighters teach people about fire safety.

The leading cause of home fires is cooking. If you cook, stay in the kitchen while food is on the stove. Turn off the stove if you leave the kitchen. The second biggest cause of home fires is heating. A space heater can start a fire if it is placed too close to objects that can burn. Kids can help prevent fires by not playing with matches or candles. And don't get too close to anything that can burn you.

In case of fire, it's important that everyone in your family knows what to do to stay safe. Here are some tips.

Plan Ahead

- Your family should draw a map of your home that shows the fastest ways out of every room, especially the bedrooms. Babysitters should also know these paths.

- Place emergency numbers next to every phone. Code 911 or an emergency number in cell phones.

- Test all smoke alarms once a month. Make sure there is one on every level of your home. Put new batteries in smoke alarms every year, and replace the alarms every 10 years.

- Clear all exit routes in your house. Take things off stairs and make sure doors and windows open easily.

- Pick a meeting place outside your home where family members can gather after they leave a burning building.

- Hold fire drills when everyone is home and hold them at different times of the day.

During a Fire

- If there is a fire, crawl or roll to the door of your room. To check if the fire is near the door, feel the doorknob with the back of your hand and the cracks around the door for heat. If the door is warm, you may have to get out another way, like through a window.

- To exit from an upper window, you need a portable escape ladder. All upper-story bedrooms should have escape ladders. Don't practice climbing down one in a drill. They should only be used in emergencies. If you don't have a ladder, hang a white or light-colored sheet out the window. That will alert firefighters that you are in the room.

FACTOID

Benjamin Franklin formed the first volunteer fire company in America in 1736, in Philadelphia, Pennsylvania. Of course, he was also the first fire chief.

DID YOU KNOW?

Dalmatians aren't just cute black and white spotted dogs in Disney movies. They have long been the watchdogs of firehouses. The reason? Fire engines were once driven by horses. Dalmatians form a close bond with horses and would protect them from horse thieves.

- Smoke rises, so get out of the house by bending down or crawling to the exit.
- Close all doors behind you.
- Never stop to take anything with you during a fire.
- Never go back into a burning building.
- When you're outside, call the fire department or emergency number.

Getting into Gear

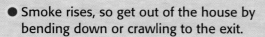 need a lot of protection when they go into a burning building. A hundred years ago, firefighters wore wool pants and shirts. Today's firefighting clothing, called turnout gear, provides better insulation. Firefighters wear several layers: One resists heat up to 1,200°F, another is water resistant, and a third is fire-resistant. The gear is so effective, firefighters sometimes don't realize how hot a fire is. New gear is solving that problem. The clothing comes with sensors that warn the firefighter when temperatures in a building are dangerously high.

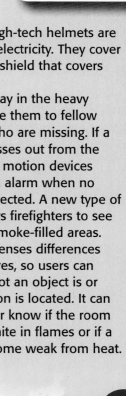

All firefighters wear helmets, and early versions were made of leather and later aluminum. Nowadays, high-tech helmets are resistant to heat, flames, and electricity. They cover the ears and neck and have a shield that covers the face.

Firefighters can lose their way in the heavy smoke. GPS devices help guide them to fellow firefighters who are missing. If a firefighter passes out from the smoke, small motion devices will set off an alarm when no motion is detected. A new type of camera allows firefighters to see in dark and smoke-filled areas. The camera senses differences in temperatures, so users can detect how hot an object is or where a person is located. It can let a firefighter know if the room is ready to ignite in flames or if a floor has become weak from heat. Hot stuff!

HOW to Stay Safe During a Tornado

The United States is twister central. More tornadoes hit the U.S. than any other country. Each year, about 1,300 touch down here.

Tornadoes come in all sizes and speeds. They can spin from 86 miles per hour to 200 miles per hour or faster. Some tornadoes measure only a few feet in diameter, while some are as wide as a mile. A tornado can last a few seconds or spin for more than an hour and travel 50 miles or more. No matter how long a tornado lasts, it can threaten lives and property. A tornado will pick up cars, trees, homes, and anything else in its path. But if you know what to do when a twister hits, you can stay safe.

FACTOID

Most twisters in the U.S. touch down in Tornado Alley. That's the nickname given to the states in the central United States. But twisters have struck every state at one time or other.

Before a Tornado Hits

- Make sure your family has a plan in place for when you are at home, at school, or outdoors.
- Hold drills so you know what to do in case a tornado approaches.
- The National Weather Service broadcasts warnings and forecasts. Know what these expressions mean:
  - Tornado Watch: Stay alert for approaching storms.
  - Tornado Warning: Go to a safe place.
  - Severe Thunderstorm Warnings: Tornadoes can form in areas hit by powerful thunderstorms.
- Check the skies for storms that are coming your way. Look for these danger signs:
  - The wind dies down suddenly, and the air becomes very still
  - Large, dark, low-lying clouds
  - A cloud of debris in the sky
  - A loud roar that sounds like a train coming in your direction
- If you see any signs of a possible tornado, take shelter right away.

During a Tornado

If you are indoors:

- Go to a sheltered area, such as a basement, storm cellar, or an inner room of the building's lowest level.
- Stay away from corners, windows, and doors. Move as far away as possible from the outside walls.
- Go under a heavy table and protect your head and neck with your arms.
- Do not open any windows.

If you are outdoors:

- Lie down in a ditch or low area and stay as flat as possible. Cover your head with your hands.
- Do not go under an overpass or bridge.
- If you are in a car or truck, leave the vehicle for shelter. Don't try to outrun a tornado.
- Watch out for flying objects.

Researchers set up equipment to gather information about a fast-approaching twister.

Spin Cycle

Tornadoes usually form during giant thunderstorms called supercells. Fast-moving winds above and slow-moving winds below set a horizontal tube of air spinning. Rising warm air tilts the tube until it is vertical. Cooler air pulls the tube to the ground. A tornado is formed. Many tornadoes are brown or black from the dust and dirt they suck up through the vortex, or center.

SUPERCELL

VORTEX

WARM AIR

COOLER AIR

HOW Does a Search Dog Find a Missing Person?

You've probably heard the old saying that dogs are a human's best friend. For members of a police force, search and rescue dogs are the best of the best. Search and rescue (SAR) canines are used to find people lost in the woods or buried under the rubble of collapsed buildings. SAR dogs are specially trained to detect human scent. They've found people buried 20 feet under snow and 40 feet underwater. The reason: A dog's nose is 10,000 times more sensitive than a human's.

SAR dogs go anywhere to help find people. These daring, brave canines are really top dogs!

Air-scent Dogs

These dogs are trained to pick up the scent of a human. People give off millions of tiny particles, including skin cells, bacteria, and sweat. Dogs can detect these particles in the air and on the ground. Air-scent dogs, such as bloodhounds, roam free in large areas to find a human scent and lead its handler to the source.

Trailing and Tracking Dogs

These dogs search for a particular person. The dog is given an object that has the person's scent, such as a comb or piece of clothing. Then, the dog sniffs out that particular scent on the ground. The scent can stick to grass, branches, and other objects.

FACTOID

SAR dogs must be trainable, able to get in and out of tight spots, have great energy, and get along with people and other dogs. They are usually large breeds, such as German shepherds, dobermans, rottweilers, golden retrievers, giant schnauzers, and labradors.

Avalanche Dogs

Some SAR dogs are trained to find people buried under snow. When oils on a person's skin warm up, their scent rises right up through snow. An avalanche dog can detect the scent above the surface of the snow and alert rescuers.

To the Rescue

Dogs aren't the only animals that give humans a helping hand, er, paw. Here are a few other critters that serve people.

Miniature Horses

They have been used as guide animals for blind people and to pull wheelchairs.

Capuchin Monkeys

These monkeys can act as the hands for people in wheelchairs or who can't get around easily. The monkeys are quick learners and can help a human for 25 to 30 years. The monkeys can use their hands to turn doorknobs or the pages of a book.

Cats

Cats, as well as dogs, are used as pet therapy for people in hospitals and nursing homes. Petting an animal can make people feel better and can lower their blood pressure.

Disaster Dogs

They are trained to find human scent like the other SAR dogs. But they must be able to move in and around rubble from collapsed buildings and other dangerous ground. The dogs can't be afraid of splinters of wood, sharp points of steel, and broken glass. Dust and noise don't bother these incredible canines.

Water Search

Some dogs sniff out humans who are in—or under—water. A person who drowns leaves cells floating on the surface of the water. The victim also gives off gases that rise to the surface. A dog can detect those smells along the shore, while in a boat, or swimming in water.

HOW to Make a Compass

It's not easy to get lost. Today, people have excellent maps and a GPS satellite system that show us where we are. A thousand years ago, people didn't have either. When they were sailing on the ocean, it was tough for them to figure out their location. Around 1100 A.D., sailors came up with a way to help them navigate: a compass. Their compass was a magnetized needle that floated in a bucket of water. Today, there are many types of compasses, but the compass used by ancient sailors can still point you in the right direction.

What You Need

- Sewing needle about one inch long
- Small bar magnet or refrigerator magnet
- Small piece of cork
- Glass or cup of water

What to Do

1 Rub the magnet against the needle in one direction for a minute or so. Make sure you move the magnet in the same direction each time.

2 Stick the needle through the center of the cork. The ends of the needle should stick out from the cork. Be careful that you don't stick yourself.

Compass Points

Magnetic compasses work because the Earth is a giant magnet. Deep in the planet's core is a molten ball of iron. The rotation of the Earth makes the liquid iron spin, which produces a magnetic field. The north end of Earth's magnetic field is located near the North Pole. The south end is near the South Pole. A compass is a magnet with a north and south end. Since opposites attract, the south end of a magnet points towards the magnetic north. The north end points to the magnetic south.

3 Put the needle and cork in the glass of water and place the glass on a table. The cork and needle should float freely, more or less parallel to the surface of the water. The glass should be wide enough so the ends of the needle don't touch the sides of the glass.

4 The needle should spin and eventually point in one direction.

5 Move the bar magnet near your compass. What happens?

Why It Happened

By rubbing the needle against the magnet, the needle became magnetized. Floating in water, the compass rotates in the direction of Earth's magnetic field. It points to either the North or South Pole, depending on which is closer to you.

Lost and Found

Even with a compass, it is possible to get lost in the woods if you're hiking. Here are some tips in case it ever happens.

- O Never go on a hike without an adult.
- O Make sure a relative or friend knows where you will be hiking.
- O If you are lost, stay in one place or area. Do not wander around looking for help—help will find you.

- O Keep warm and dry while waiting for someone to come for you. Cover up your exposed skin. Wear a hat to keep your head warm.
- O Stay together with the other hikers. You can hold on to each other to keep warm.
- O Find a comfortable place to stay that will keep you out of wind and rain. Wait under a large tree, for example, where searchers can easily see you.
- O Attract attention. Wear something bright to stand out. Try to make a flag out of any light-colored paper, ribbon, or other objects you have.
- O Do not lie down on the bare ground. The cold ground will drop your body temperature. To stay warm, cover the ground and yourself with a thick layer of branches, moss, or leaves.
- O Don't eat anything in the woods. It's better to be hungry than sick.

HOW to Make a Survival Kit

Hurricanes, floods, earthquakes, tornadoes, fires. Each year, disasters affect thousands of people. And when trouble hits, the Federal Emergency Management Agency (FEMA) comes to the rescue. The U.S. agency's job is to find places to live for people who have lost their homes due to disasters. FEMA helps repair homes and fixes public buildings that have been damaged. It provides supplies, workers, and equipment to a community that has been hit hard by nature's fury.

FEMA also trains firefighters and other emergency workers before a problem occurs so they will be ready to help out. The agency suggests that families should have a survival kit that is kept in a safe place. Here is what FEMA says should be in the kit—because it's always good to be prepared.

A Helping Hand

FEMA is one of many organizations that helps the victims of disasters and emergencies. Here are a few others:

American Red Cross provides emergency aid including food stations, shelter, first aid, clothing, home repairs, and medical supplies. They are on the scene when other relief assistance isn't enough.

Children's Disaster Response trains volunteers who help children after disasters. They work with parents, community agencies, and schools to help them understand the needs of children.

Friends Disaster Service helps the elderly, the disabled, and people who don't have much money or insurance after a disaster.

Mennonite Disaster Services provides volunteers to clean up and remove rubble from damaged homes and to help repair the houses.

National Emergency Response Team helps out disaster victims by providing trailers that house eight to 10 people.

Three-Day Survival Kit

Store at least one gallon of water per person per day. Buy bottled water and don't open it until you need it.

Store a supply of canned food and a non-electric can opener. You should not have to refrigerate, cook, or add water to these foods. Choose cans that are small and light. Don't choose foods that make you thirsty. And don't forget your vitamins.

Include a first-aid kit that contains such basics as adhesive bandages, scissors, antiseptic, safety pins, soap, aspirin, and anti-bacteria cream.

Store warm clothing. There should be at least one complete change of clothes for each person, including rain gear, sturdy shoes, and gloves.

Include sanitation items, such as toilet paper, liquid detergent, a plastic bucket with a tight lid, disinfectant, toothbrushes, and toothpaste.

Store tools, such as paper plates and cups, a battery-powered radio, a flashlight, extra batteries, a fire extinguisher, and plastic storage containers.

Keep important family documents in a waterproof container, including IDs, family records, credit card numbers, and important telephone numbers.

Don't forget some fun stuff, such as games and books.

HOW Do Bicycle Gears Make You Go Faster?

A bicycle is a great way to get around. It doesn't pollute, it's easy to ride, it's good exercise, and it's fun. One of the best things about a bike is that you can make the ride smoother with the press of a lever. What allows you to get in gear is, well, the gears.

A gear is a wheel with teeth that stick out. A bicycle has two sets of gears. One set is connected to the pedal, the other is attached to the rear wheel. A 3-speed bike has 3 gears, or "speeds." A mountain bike might have 24 gears. These gears let you change the distance the bike travels forward each time you turn the pedals. The higher the gear you put the bike in, the more distance you can travel with each turn of the pedals—and the faster you can go.

The gears are wheels with teeth, or cogs, that fit into the chain. As the gears move, so does the chain.

The back gears are turned by the chain. As the gears turn, so does the back wheel.

The rear derailer (derailleur) changes the back gears by moving the chain from gear to gear.

The crank turns the front gears.

The chain connects the front and rear gears.

Top athletes need to know the newest technologies, the best equipment for their sport, and the right moves. But you don't need to be a pro to learn some awesome sports skills.

Gearing Up

The higher the gear, the farther the bike goes each time it's pedaled. If the front gear on a bike is twice as big as the rear gear, the rear wheel will turn two times each time you pedal once. If the front gear is three times bigger than the back gear, the back wheel will turn three times for each turn of the pedals.

Bicyclists have to pedal harder in high gears, but they can go faster. Riders use high gears to go down hills or speed up on straightaways. In lower gears, riders don't need to pedal as hard, but they can't go as fast as in high gear. Riders use low gears to go up hills.

The **front derailer (derailleur)** changes the front gears by moving the chain from one gear to another.

The **pedals** turn the crank.

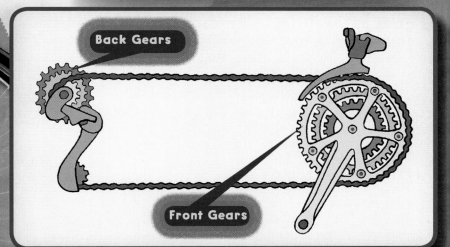

Back Gears

Front Gears

HOW Are Baseball Bats Made?

When major league baseball players grab a bat in the dugout, more often than not it's a Louisville Slugger. Louisville Sluggers are a big hit with ballplayers—and they have been since the company Hillerich & Bradsby began making wood bats in 1884 in Louisville, Kentucky.

There are dozens of bat companies in the U.S., Canada, and Japan. But Hillerich & Bradsby is the most famous. Over the years, it has sold more than 100,000,000 bats. It sends about 200,000 bats to the pros each year. More than 60 percent of major league players use Louisville Sluggers, including Derek Jeter and Evan Longoria. To learn how bats are made, you have to head home. Not to home plate, but to the home of the Louisville Slugger.

FACTOID

About half of all major league bats produced by Hillerich & Bradsby are made from ash trees, and the other half are made from maple trees. The company grows the trees in forests they own in Pennsylvania and New York.

1 Every Louisville Slugger starts out as a log cut from trees at one of three mills in the Northeast U.S. One tree can produce 35 to 40 bats. Inside the mill, machines remove bark from the logs, which are cut into 40-inch-long sections.

3 Major league equipment managers send in orders for bats. Players choose specific types of wood (ash or maple), shape, length, weight, color, and finish. A machine controlled by a computer shapes the billet into the correct bat model.

2

The logs are cut into 18 to 20 smaller tubes, called billets. Billets are damp, so they are dried out in an oven for four to five weeks. The billets are cut down to 37 inches, then shipped to the Louisville Slugger factory in Kentucky.

KEELER, N. Y. AMER.

5

4

A player can have his signature stamped on the bat with oil dyes. Or the signature can be burned on with a metal brand heated to 1,400°F. Machines then sand the bat and cut off the knobs, which were used to hold the bat in place.

If a bat is colored, it is dipped in paint and hung to dry. Once the bat stops dripping, a special light dries it further for 15 minutes. Now it's ready to be shipped to stadiums around the U.S. and Canada. An average pro player will go through about 100 bats each season.

HOW Does Hockey Equipment Keep Players Safe?

Ice hockey is a cool sport. It's also a rough game. Professional players can skate at speeds of more than 20 miles per hour. That's almost as fast as the fastest sprinters in the world. When skaters collide, bodies often crash against wood and glass boards surrounding the rink, or fall on hard ice. Players also shoot rubber pucks that can hit players. The hardest shots send the puck at speeds of 100 miles per hour. Players can get cut and poked by hockey sticks and skates. To avoid injury, ice hockey players cover themselves from head to toe in protective equipment. After all, staying safe should be every player's goal.

Mouthguard: Plastic guard that fits over the teeth. This helps protect the teeth from flying pucks and hockey sticks.

Gloves: Protect hands against an opponent's stick, the puck, and the sharp edge of skate blades. The outer part and finger area are thickly padded. The inner side is thinner, so players can feel and control the stick.

Skates: The outside of the shoe is a rigid shell, sometimes with metal mesh built inside it. This stops a skate blade from cutting through the shoe. The heel of the skate is rounded, not sharp, so it won't cut other players.

FACTOID

In most youth hockey leagues, players can't raise their sticks high or play too roughly. Hitting, or checking, another player with the body is not allowed.

Helmet: A hard plastic shell protects the head. Many helmets come with a plastic shield that covers the eyes and upper part of the face or a wire mask, or cage, that covers the whole face. Some helmets have a shield and a cage.

Shoulder and chest padding: Protect the collarbone, shoulders, chest, and upper arms and back. They are made of very hard plastic sewn onto foam-padded cloth. Some have extra pieces that protect the stomach area and lower back.

Pants: Inside are pads of cloth and plastic to protect parts of the leg, hip, and lower back.

Shin guards: Made of plastic, they protect the knee and the lower leg, right down to the foot.

The Man in the Mask

With pucks flying at them at 100 miles per hour, what goalie wouldn't wear a face mask? Well, before 1959, no goalies did. The first to wear one in a game was Montreal Canadiens goalie Jacques Plante. At the time, people thought he wasn't very brave. Eventually, all goalies began to wear masks. Over the years, they have gotten larger to protect more of the goalie's head and throat. Players also decorate their masks. Here are some masks that have been worn through the years.

● The first mask, worn by Jacques Plante, was made of fiberglass and was held on by a strap.

● Early masks got bigger, to cover more of the goalie's face and head. Padding was also added.

● Goalies had trouble seeing out of their masks—until Soviet goaltender Vladislav Tretiak showed them how. The front of his mask was covered by a metal cage. Because the cage wasn't touching the face, being hit by a puck didn't hurt as much.

● In the 1970s, players began painting their masks. Today, the masks are like works of art.

HOW Do You Do a Skateboard Trick Called an Ollie?

In the 1950s, California surfers needed something fun to ride when there were no waves. So they invented the skateboard. The first skateboards looked more like scooters than today's models. They were made of metal roller skate wheels attached to a wooden board or box. Skateboarding didn't really take off as a sport until 1973. In that year, plastic wheels were first attached to skateboards.

Thanks to plastic wheels, skaters could go faster and do cool tricks, such as skating on two wheels (wheelies), spinning on the back wheels (pivot), or jumping over a bar and landing back on the board (hippie jump). In 1976, a skater from Florida named Allan "Ollie" Gelfand invented a trick that let the skater pop the skateboard into the air. Gelfand's invention opened the way for many mid-air tricks. His trick is the one most beginning skateboarders learn first: the ollie.

FROM TFK

Q&A with Tony Hawk

Many consider **Tony Hawk** the greatest skateboarder of all time. TIME FOR KIDS asked him some questions.

TFK: What did you feel when you started out as a young skater?
Hawk: When I first went to the skate park, and I saw what was really possible—these guys were flying out of empty swimming pools—I was like, "I want to do that. I want to fly." So then I started going to skate parks on a regular basis. Every time I went, I would learn something new.

TFK: What advice do you have for beginning skaters?
Hawk: Take it slow. It takes repeated attempts to learn a kick flip and to develop skills. And you've got to work at it.

TFK: What advice do you have for kids who hope to achieve success?
Hawk: Do what you love doing, even if it doesn't seem like it's the coolest thing at the time. If you enjoy it, you have to follow it, because ultimately you're going to be happy going to work every day.

1

Put your front foot near the middle of the board, about two inches from where the bolt is. Your back foot should be on the tail, or back, of the board.

2

Bend both your legs and squat down. You should be ready to jump.

3

Slide the side of your front foot to the front of the board. At the same time, push down hard on the tail with your back foot. Your back leg should straighten as the tail hits the ground.

4

When the board is in the air, stop moving your front foot. Pull your knees up toward your chest. Raise your back foot so the board can rise until it is fairly level in the air.

5

When the board is level in the air and it begins to drop, straighten your legs.

6

As you land, bend your legs to absorb the shock. The board should be level as it lands, so all the wheels touch ground at the same time. Both feet should be over the bolts. Your back foot should not be over the tail. Don't try this on a moving skateboard until you have the trick down.

FACTOID

Tony Hawk is the king of skateboarders. Before quitting competitive skateboarding in 1999, he won 73 skateboarding contests, invented many tricks, and was the first skater to land a "900:" two-and-a-half spins in mid-air while on a board.

HOW Do You Do the Snowboarding Trick Called Butter?

Do you like to shred? No, not cutting paper into small pieces. Shred is slang for snowboarding, a sport that's like skiing, but on one board and with no poles. Modern snowboarding was invented in 1965 by Sherman Poppen. He tied two cheap skis together and surfed down snow: He snurfed. When a better version of a snowboard was introduced a few years later, the sport became as popular as skateboarding.

Snowboarders jump, spin, and do wild mid-air tricks. Because a snowboarder's feet are attached to the board, jumps are easier to make. But you can do plenty of on-the-ground snowboarding tricks. One of the most basic moves is called butter, which lets a boarder easily spin in a complete circle. Butter can be done at low speed and on flat snow. When you finally have it down, it's, um, snow good!

Beautiful Boards

Snowboards not only go fast, they look great. The artwork on snowboards makes them really stand out in the snow. Here are a few awesome examples.

1 Find a flat, smooth, empty area to practice. The snowboard should be flat against the snow.

2 Put most of your weight on your front foot. Raise your back foot to lift the board off the snow. Don't lift it too high or you'll lose your balance.

3 As the board's tail rises, rotate your body, using your front foot as a pivot. Swing your back foot around until you face the opposite direction.

4 Once you've turned 180 degrees, put the tail of the board down.

5 Without raising the board, press your rear foot down hard on the snow. Rotate your body so the board spins on the ground back to your original position.

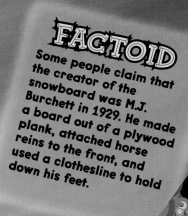

FACTOID

Some people claim that the creator of the snowboard was M.J. Burchett in 1929. He made a board out of a plywood plank, attached horse reins to the front, and used a clothesline to hold down his feet.

HOW Do Ice Skaters Spin So Fast?

When figure skaters glide onto the ice, they perform beautiful jumps, twists, and turns. One of the most exciting parts of a skating program is the spins. Skaters start their spins slowly and end up looking like a blur. The faster a skater spins, the more she wows the audience—and the judges. There are all kinds of spins. In one kind, the skater spins in a sitting position. In another, she stays upright and may bend her back. In a spin called the camel, the skater spins on one leg while the other leg sticks straight out in a horizontal position.

Some skaters spin faster than others. They look like they're digging a hole in the ice! Swiss skating great Lucinda Ruh set a world record in 2003 for spinning 155 times on one foot—without stopping! Skater Robbie Robertson could spin at 500 revolutions per minute. That's how he got his nickname: "The Blur."

1 When the skater starts spinning, her arms or legs are held away from the body. That is like the Earth rotating on its axis. The axis of the skater is the vertical line that goes from the top of her head to the blade of the skate.

2 The skater begins to move her legs towards her body. That's because the closer the arms and legs are to the body, or axis, the faster she spins.

FACTOID

The largest outdoor ice rink in the world is located in Japan. The Fujikyu Highland Promenade Rink has an ice area of 165,750 square feet—equal to 3.8 acres.

3

She spins fastest when her arms and legs are tight against the body. Figure skaters control the exact speed of the spin by carefully controlling the movements of their arms and legs.

4

The skater slows and eventually stops the spin by letting her arms and legs move back out. The farther they are from the axis, the slower she spins.

One Good Turn

You don't have to have a pair of skates and an ice rink to increase your spinning speed. All you need is a swivel chair.

1. Adjust the seat of the chair as high as it goes. Sit in the chair with your arms stretched out to the side.

2. Start spinning the chair with your feet, or have a friend spin the chair—but not too fast.

3. Slowly move your arms over your head. What happens?

The Dizzy Factor

Spin around in place really fast and you get dizzy. You can hardly stand up. So how do figure skaters not get dizzy and not fall down when they spin 30 or 40 times in a few seconds? Well, most skaters do get dizzy. In professional ice skating, there is a small light at both ends of the rink. This helps a dizzy skater figure out where she is at the end of the spin. Some skaters say they just get used to the dizziness. After a while, it doesn't bother them. One skater says that if everything around him is a blur, he is less aware of the spin and doesn't get dizzy. Others just enjoy spinning—they think it's relaxing!

HOW Do You Stay Upright on a Surfboard?

Hang ten. Surf's up. Gnarly. Stoked. Surfing has given the world a lot of awesome terms. That's because surfing is a totally tubular sport. It's also a difficult skill to learn and master.

Catching a wave and riding it to shore isn't easy. The surfer's goal is to stay standing on the surfboard for as long as possible. Surfers do this by staying ahead of the white water of the wave—the part that crashes down. Some waves form a tube as they break. Experienced surfboarders like to ride inside the tube so they are surrounded by water. They know how to ride out of the tube before several tons of ocean fall on them. It takes years to become an expert surfer. But the first step is learning how to stand up on a board.

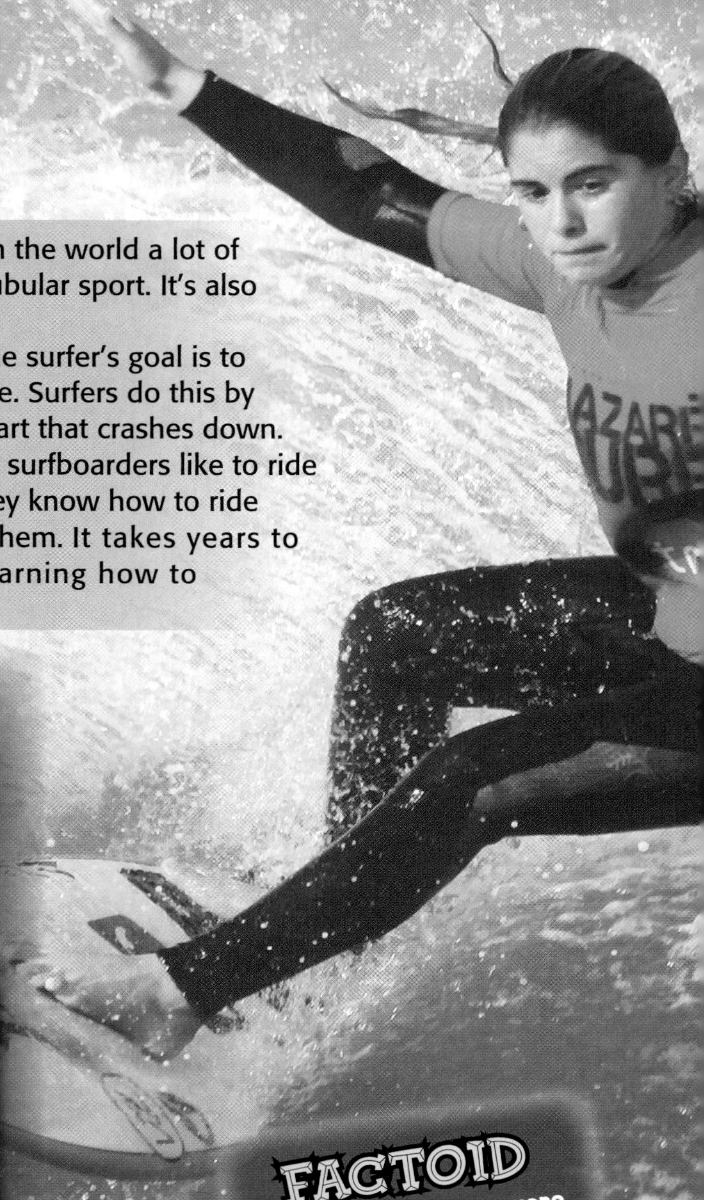

Catching Big Waves

Big-wave surfers are surfers who seek out monster waves, often between 20 to 40 feet high—like the one shown here at Pipeline beach in Oahu, Hawaii. The biggest wave ever surfed was 70 feet high, ridden by Pete Cabrinha in 2006.

FACTOID

The original surfers were Polynesians in the islands of the Pacific Ocean. They first rode wooden boards on waves about 3,000 years ago.

Surf's Up!

Standing up on a surfboard on water isn't easy. So practice on the beach or other dry land. First, figure out which position is more comfortable: right foot forward or left foot forward. Lay the board on a flat surface. Use a board that doesn't have fins.

1

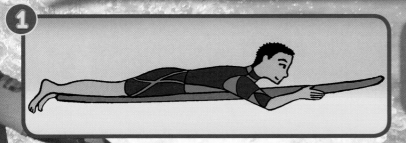

Lie stomach down on the board. You shouldn't be too far forward on the board. Stretch out your arms and hold the rails, or sides of the board.

2

Slide your hands back until they reach the level of your shoulders. Do a push up: extend your arms to push your body up.

3

4

Get into a crouch. If you are a righty, bring your left foot forward. If you are a lefty, move your right foot forward. Your front knee should be lined up with your chin.

Stand up slowly, but not all the way. Keep your forward foot in the same position. Move your back foot so it's a few feet from the front foot. Remember: Don't try this in water unless you've first taken lessons at a good surf school.

HOW Can You Prevent Sports Injuries?

Playing sports is fun, but not if you overdo it. Young athletes often injure their bones, muscles, and tendons (tissue that attaches muscles to bones). A lot of these injuries are caused when an athlete puts stress on the same body parts over and over. This often happens when they play one sport and play it year round. By the time young athletes are in middle or high school, nearly half of their injuries are caused by the wear and tear of overuse.

Athletes also get overuse injuries when they play different sports that stress the same body parts. Basketball and soccer players often have trouble with their knees. Divers, cheerleaders, gymnasts, and football players may develop back problems. Baseball and tennis players risk injuries to their elbows. For young athletes, a little variety and not overdoing it are good things.

On these pages are four common sports injuries young athletes get.

Baseball

Little League elbow: Slight tears and inflammation of tendons and ligaments in the inner elbow

Cause: Throwing too hard and too often, especially curve balls

Warning signs: A painful or stiff elbow when throwing a ball, difficulty holding arm out straight, pain when gripping or carrying heavy objects

Prevention: Kids ages 9–12 should not pitch more than four innings per game and six innings a week. Stop throwing curve balls.

Soccer

Sever disease: An inflammation of the back of the foot where the heel bone attaches to the Achilles tendon

Cause: Overuse of bone and tendons in the heel

Warning signs: One or both heels hurt while walking, running, or jumping.

Prevention: Gently stretch calf muscles daily and before games. Wear sports shoes with strong arch supports. Don't walk or run in bare feet.

Basketball, Volleyball, and Bicycling

Jumper's knee: An inflammation of the tendon that attaches the kneecap to the shin bone

Cause: Frequent jumping or doing intense activity that puts stress on the knees

Warning signs: Pain just below the kneecap that increases during physical activity, especially running or jumping

Prevention: Warm up before games. Let your coach know if you feel pain in knees. Rest between games or stop playing until pain goes away.

Running

Shin splints: An inflammation of muscles or tendons attached to the shin bone

Cause: Running downhill or on a slanted surface, running too hard, too fast, or too long

Warning signs: Pain, soreness, tenderness, and sometimes slight swelling along the front edge of the shin

Prevention: Run before season and slowly increase distance. Do not sprint while running for distance. Wear proper running shoes. Stretch calf and ankle muscles before and after competitions.

Sports Kids Play

Do you play hoops, baseball, soccer? A poll of more than 1,000 kids reveals what their favorite sports to play are.

1. Basketball........ 30 %
2. Baseball .... 20.9 %
3. Football .... 20.8 %
4. Hockey .... 9.8 %
5. Soccer .... 9.1 %

Source: Sports Illustrated Kids

FACTOID

According to the National Council of Youth Sports, 44 million children take part in youth sports in the U.S. Sixty-six percent are boys and 34 percent are girls.

HOW Does an Arena Change an Ice Rink into a Basketball Court?

Ice hockey and basketball couldn't be more different. Hockey players bang into each other as they skate on ice. Basketball players run and jump on a wooden floor.

Even though the games and playing surfaces are very different, the sports are often played in the same arena—and on the same day! How do workers make the changeover? Here's how it works in the STAPLES Center, located in Los Angeles, California.

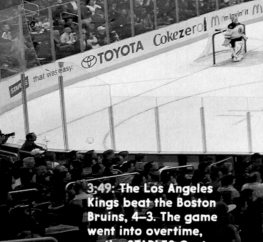

3:49: The Los Angeles Kings beat the Boston Bruins, 4–3. The game went into overtime, so the STAPLES Center workers have less time than usual to get ready for an NBA game, which is set to start in less than four hours.

3:59: The crew first takes down the glass around the rink. Forklifts help remove the glass and the pieces that hold the glass in place. Then workers begin to cover the ice with more than 600 panels, which protect the ice surface and help keep it frozen.

4:38: After workers cover the floor with panels, they put down the basketball floor. They start at center court and build outward. The basketball court is made of 217 pieces. The pieces are numbered and come out stacked on top of one another.

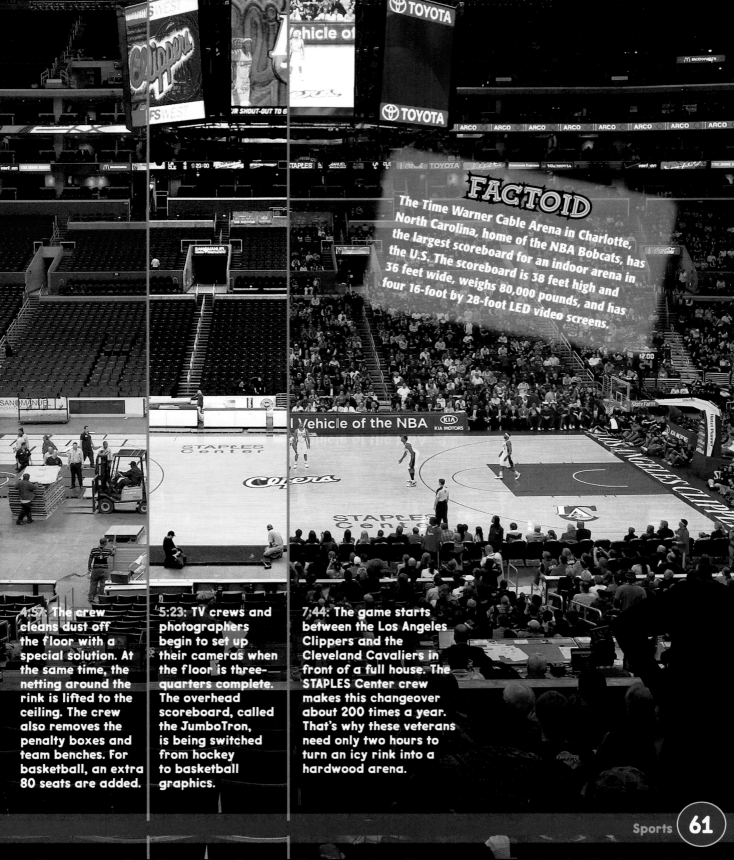

FACTOID

The Time Warner Cable Arena in Charlotte, North Carolina, home of the NBA Bobcats, has the largest scoreboard for an indoor arena in the U.S. The scoreboard is 38 feet high and 36 feet wide, weighs 80,000 pounds, and has four 16-foot by 28-foot LED video screens.

4:57: The crew cleans dust off the floor with a special solution. At the same time, the netting around the rink is lifted to the ceiling. The crew also removes the penalty boxes and team benches. For basketball, an extra 80 seats are added.

5:23: TV crews and photographers begin to set up their cameras when the floor is three-quarters complete. The overhead scoreboard, called the JumboTron, is being switched from hockey to basketball graphics.

7:44: The game starts between the Los Angeles Clippers and the Cleveland Cavaliers in front of a full house. The STAPLES Center crew makes this changeover about 200 times a year. That's why these veterans need only two hours to turn an icy rink into a hardwood arena.

HOW Does Motion Capture Technology Help Athletes?

Motion capture technology is a way to make a computer-generated figure look incredibly lifelike. In motion capture, a person's movements are captured by cameras, recorded by a computer, and turned into a 3-D animation of that person. Motion capture plays a major role in movies and in sports video games.

Now motion capture is capturing the imagination of sports teams. Motion capture is helping some major league baseball teams see what caused, or may cause, an injury to a pitcher. It is also used to improve a player's performance.

A coach can compare the motion capture version of a baseball player when he is hitting well and when he is in a slump. Motion capture is also a tool to help athletes train.

A football team might create a motion capture animation of its linemen. Then a football player wearing 3-D glasses can practice against these life-size animated teammates. Best of all, there's no chance of getting injured!

1

To make a motion capture of a pitcher, researchers attach 75 small globes, called markers, to different parts of his body. Above the pitcher are 20 high-speed cameras that capture him as he goes through his pitching motion. Each camera shoots out infrared rays that bounce off the moving markers and get recorded in the camera.

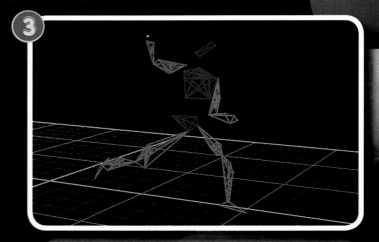

3

A software program connects the dots. Now the pitcher looks like a three-dimensional doll. The markers on the fingers, wrists, and shoulders are made to look like the doll's arm. It doesn't look like the pitcher, but it moves just like him.

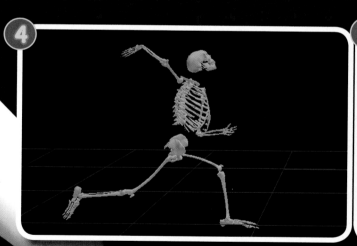

2

The images in the camera are sent into a computer. On the computer screen the player looks like a moving cloud of dots against a black background. Each dot is a marker.

Capturing Stars

From soccer to skateboarding, sports video games are using motion capture to make the animation more real than ever. To imitate the signature moves of famous players, video-game makers are giving more and more sports stars the motion capture treatment. Boston Red Sox second baseman Dustin Pedroia has been motion captured, and so have many NBA players, from Gilbert Arenas to Chris Paul.

Some athletes have to really work out in front of the motion-capture cameras. Hockey player Rick Nash took 50 different shots on goal in a session. A group of English soccer players produced 150 different moves a day over five days. The results are worth the effort. Some games are so realistic, pro players watch them to pick up tips on how to improve their own—real—game.

4

Researchers can make the image look like a skeleton. It lets them see the stresses placed on the body's joints when the pitcher throws the ball.

5

Researchers can also make the image look like a video-game version of the pitcher, complete with uniform and baseball cap. This makes the animated player's movements clearer to the athlete and coach.

HOW to Make a High-Bounce Ball

How are soccer balls, baseballs, basketballs, tennis balls, and super balls alike—besides being round? Answer: They all bounce. But how come a ball bounces? And why doesn't it keep bouncing forever when you drop it?

As an object drops, it picks up energy, called kinetic energy. When an object stops falling, it has stored, or potential, energy. As a ball drops, it builds up kinetic energy. When it hits the ground, this energy causes the ball to flatten. While the ball is motionless for an instant on the ground, it has potential energy. As it springs back to its original shape, it releases the stored energy as kinetic energy. So the ball bounces. No ball can bounce back to its original height (although the Super Ball comes close). The ball loses energy each time it hits the ground. And air resistance wastes more energy. Out of energy, the ball dribbles to a stop.

FACTOID

The largest Super Ball was the size of a bowling ball. It was accidentally dropped out of a hotel window in Australia. The ball bounced up 15 stories and came down on a parked car, destroying it.

What You Need

- 4-ounce bottle of white, school glue
- 1-pint glass jar
- 1 ½ cups distilled water
- Food coloring (any color)
- 2-quart bowl
- 1 teaspoon borax powder (a laundry detergent found in the supermarket)

What to Do

1 Pour the bottle of glue into the jar.

2 Fill the now-empty glue bottle with ½ cup distilled water. Then pour the water from the glue bottle into the jar.

3 Put 10 drops of food coloring into the jar and stir.

4 Pour the remaining distilled water into the bowl. With a parent, add the borax powder. Stir until the powder dissolves.

5 While stirring, slowly pour the glue into the bowl containing the borax.

6 Take the glue mixture out of the bowl. Push and pull on it until it's smooth and dry. Roll it into a ball and make it bounce.

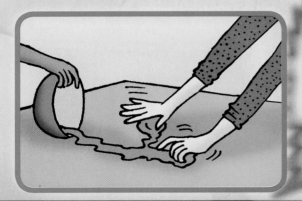

How the Ball Bounces

Some people call it a bouncy ball. Others call it a power ball or super ball. Whatever the name, it's the bounciest ball ever. The original Super Ball was invented by Norman H. Stingley in 1965. He took some rubber, added a few ingredients, and heated it up under great pressure. Wham-O, the company that sold the Frisbee, produced the first Super Balls. Now many companies make these bodacious bouncers.

Some people claim a Super Ball is so elastic, it will bounce for a minute even if it's dropped from a short height. The first bounce of a Super Ball reaches more than 80 percent of the height it was dropped from. That's three times the height that a tennis ball reaches. When it first came out, people would slam a Super Ball on the concrete and watch it bounce higher than a three-story apartment.

What Happened

Fluids can be thin and flow easily. Or they can be thick and flow more slowly. The measure of a fluid's ability to flow is called viscosity (vis-*kos*-eh-tee). The thickness of some fluids changes when you apply a force. You applied force to the goopy mixture when you pulled and pushed it. This thickened the goop so it couldn't flow easily.

HOW to Find the Sweet Spot on a Bat

When hitters get "good wood" on a ball, they're hitting the ball on the "sweet spot" of the bat. It's the spot that makes a ball go farthest.

When a player hits a ball on the sweet spot, most of the energy the two moving objects produce goes into sending the ball towards the seats. If you hit the ball anywhere else on the bat, the bat will vibrate from head to handle. These vibrations waste energy, so less energy is transferred to the ball. The ball won't go as far as when it's hit off the sweet spot. Vibrations sometimes cause another problem. If you've ever hit a baseball off the handle of the bat, you know the vibrations can sting your hands!

What You Need
- Baseball bat
- Baseball
- Pencil
- A friend

What to Do

1 Between thumb and index finger, hold a bat about halfway down the handle. (Hold an aluminum bat about one-quarter of the way down the handle.) The barrel of the bat should point down.

2 Tap a baseball against the bat, right below the fingers holding it. The bat should vibrate.

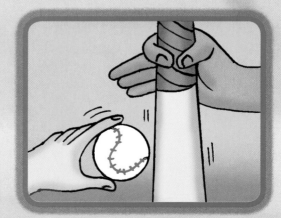

DID YOU KNOW?

Some players have "corked" their wood bats. They hollowed out the barrel and put cork, bouncy balls, or other light materials into the hole. Players believed that they could swing the bat faster and create more power. Corked bats are not allowed in Major League Baseball.

3. Keep tapping the bat, moving down the barrel. Find the spot where the tapping doesn't make the bat vibrate. Mark the spot on the bat with a pencil. This is the sweet spot.

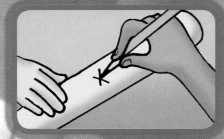

4. Hold the bat straight out in front of you, in a horizontal position. Have a friend drop a baseball onto the bat from about a foot above it.

5. Drop it at different points along the bat. The ball will bounce highest at the sweet spot.

Going, Going, Gone?

When big leaguers come to the plate, they swing lumber. Only wood bats are allowed in the major and minor leagues. But in many youth leagues, players can use metal bats. And that worries some people.

Young players like metal bats because they let kids hit the ball harder. Metal bats are hollow, which makes them lighter than wood bats. This makes it possible for hitters to swing the bats faster. Also, metal bats are more flexible than wood, which causes the ball to bounce off them with greater force. There is worry that balls hit off metal bats travel so fast, they can injure infielders, especially pitchers.

Some people want metal bats outlawed. Others say metal bats don't cause any more injuries than wood ones. They also point to the cost. Wood bats break and have to be replaced. Metal bats, although more expensive, last much longer. Defenders of metal bats say players should wear more protective equipment. Or the fields used by young Little Leaguers, which are smaller than regulation, should be made bigger. That way, fielders will have time to duck. The debate continues. What do you think?

FACTOID

Not even Babe Ruth could have swung this bat. The largest bat in the world is 120 feet long and weighs 68,000 pounds. The six-story-tall steel bat is located outside the Louisville Slugger Museum & Factory in Louisville, Kentucky.

Chapter ④ Buildings

HOW Were the Egyptian Pyramids Built?

The first pyramid was built in Egypt about 4,000 years ago. Pyramids were tombs for the kings of Egypt, called pharaohs. Hundreds of pyramids were built, and more than 100 still survive. The most famous are in Giza, outside of Cairo, the capital of Egypt.

It took thousands of people and a great deal of skill to build the pyramids. A small town was constructed near the pyramid site to house all workers and officials in charge, as well as the people who supplied them with food and materials. Carpenters made tools and built sleds to haul heavy loads. Metal workers created cutting tools and kept them sharp. Potters formed pots used to prepare food and carry water. Bakers were needed to bake bread for the workers. All these people worked together to build the world's first skyscrapers.

1. Pyramids were built mostly from limestone. The stone was dug out of a quarry, or large open pit. Each block of stone weighed several tons.

2. Before construction began, the base of the pyramid was measured off and sand was removed from the site. A platform, built out of limestone, served as the pyramid's foundation.

3. Groups of men hauled the blocks from the quarry to the pyramid site. They used ropes and levers made of wood to lift the blocks onto heavy sleds. If the quarry was far from the pyramid, workers or oxen would pull the sleds to the Nile River. There, barges would carry the blocks to the building site.

Humans are builders. Over thousands of years, people have created ever larger, more amazing structures. From tombs to canals, these engineering wonders continue to amaze us.

Making a Point!

Egypt wasn't the only nation to build pyramids. The shape proved popular with some ancient civilizations.

6. Workers placed a capstone, a small pyramid-shaped stone, at the top of the pyramid. It might have been covered with gold or another shiny metal to reflect the rays of the sun.

5. The central core of the pyramid was made of stones that formed steps. The space between the steps was filled in by small soft stones. A layer of fine limestone rock was placed against the small stones to make the outside of the pyramid smooth. This outer layer was removed centuries ago, and the stone was used to build Cairo.

Mexico
The **Pyramid of the Sun** is located not far from Mexico City. The vast structure was built by an ancient people of Mexico called the Teotihuacanos (tay-oh-tee-wha-*cahn*-oz) nearly 2,000 years ago. At 246 feet tall and 733 feet wide on each side, it is the third largest pyramid in the world.

India
There are many Hindu temples shaped like pyramids in India. One, the **Brihadeeswara Temple** in Thanjavur, was built in the 11th century. Made of granite, the temple tower is 216 feet high.

4. Blocks were hauled up ramps onto the pyramid. There might have been a single long ramp or many smaller ones. Ramps may have zigzagged up the sides of the pyramid or gone straight up each side. No one knows for sure.

HOW Was Mount Rushmore Built?

The four heads carved on Mount Rushmore, located in the Black Hills of South Dakota, are big shots in every way. The heads of Presidents George Washington, Thomas Jefferson, Theodore Roosevelt, and Abraham Lincoln are each 60 feet tall. Their features are huge: Each nose is 20 feet long, the mouths are 18 feet wide, and each eye is 11 feet across. If their bodies were built to scale, they would be 46 stories high.

During the summer, more than 20,000 visitors come each day to admire the humongous monument. Sculptor Gutzon Borglum began the project in 1927, and it was completed in 1941. During that time, 450,000 tons of granite, a type of stone, was removed from Mount Rushmore, mostly by dynamite. Those explosives helped create one of the largest works of art in the world.

1. Mount Rushmore was picked because the rock could be easily carved. Also, the mountainside received a lot of sunlight, so visitors could view it for most of the day.

6. As Mount Rushmore neared completion in 1941, workers used hammers and chisels to smooth the rock faces.

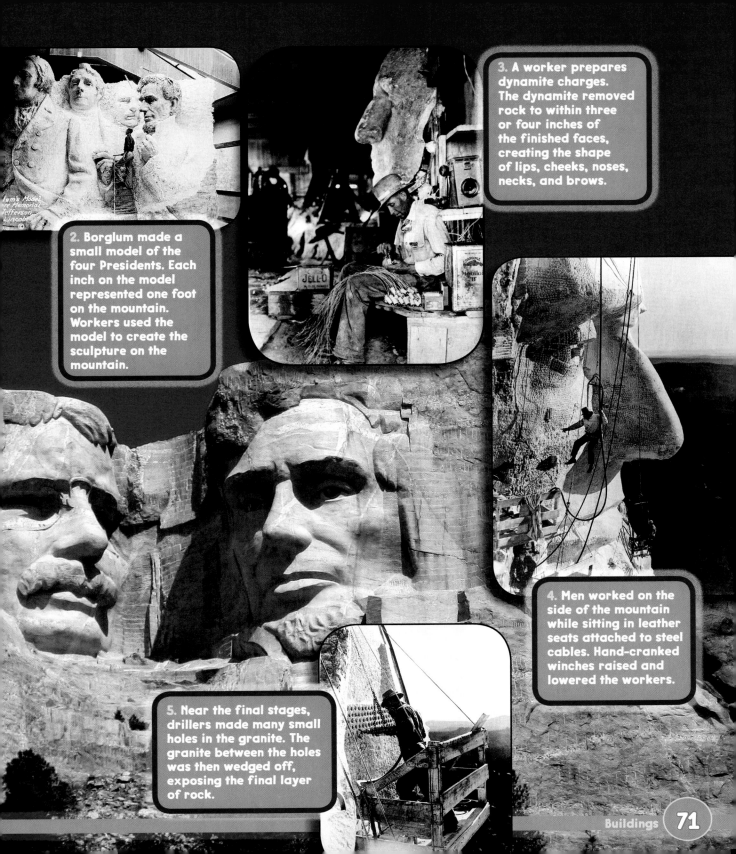

3. A worker prepares dynamite charges. The dynamite removed rock to within three or four inches of the finished faces, creating the shape of lips, cheeks, noses, necks, and brows.

2. Borglum made a small model of the four Presidents. Each inch on the model represented one foot on the mountain. Workers used the model to create the sculpture on the mountain.

4. Men worked on the side of the mountain while sitting in leather seats attached to steel cables. Hand-cranked winches raised and lowered the workers.

5. Near the final stages, drillers made many small holes in the granite. The granite between the holes was then wedged off, exposing the final layer of rock.

HOW Does the Panama Canal Work?

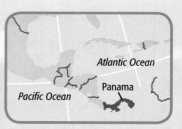

Atlantic Ocean
Panama
Pacific Ocean

The Panama Canal is one big ditch. This 300-foot-wide, 51-mile-long gash cutting through the nation of Panama, in Central America, connects the Atlantic and Pacific Oceans. Before the canal was completed in 1914, ships had to travel around the tip of South America to go from New York to San Francisco. The Panama Canal cuts that trip by 8,000 miles.

Most of the Panama Canal is above sea level. So ships that pass through it must be raised and lowered by a series of devices called locks. Today, about 14,000 ships sail through the Panama Canal each year. Some modern ships are too wide to fit in the canal. Panama is hoping to fix the canal so super-tankers and other hefty vessels can squeeze through it.

1. A ship that enters the Panama Canal from the Atlantic Ocean begins its journey at Limon Bay.

Atlantic Ocean

3. The water that pours into the Panama Canal's locks flows from Gatun Lake through special pipes. The ship is at its highest point as it sails about 23 miles on the lake.

2. The ship sails at sea level for 6.5 miles to the Gatun locks. There, three separate chambers raise the ship about 85 feet. Now the ship is at the level of Gatun Lake.

4. From Gatun Lake the ship enters the Gaillard Cut, an eight-mile-long channel.

How a Lock Works

When a ship is raised in a canal, it enters a lock. Locks are giant compartments made of thick concrete walls with huge metal doors at each end. One door opens for the ship to enter and closes behind it. Water flows into the compartment, and the ship rises with it. The water continues to flood the lock until it is at the same level as the higher lock ahead of it. Then the front door opens and the ship sails through it into the next lock. Each lock lifts the ship higher and higher. Ships are lowered in locks, too. When a ship enters a lock, the water is pumped out until the ship is at a lower level. Other locks lower the ship more and more.

Miraflores Lake

Pacific Ocean

FACTOID

The Panama Canal was a great—but difficult—building feat. Blasting away rock with dynamite was dangerous. There were accidents with trains carrying equipment. Sometimes the sides of the canal would cave in, burying weeks of work in seconds. And mosquitoes spread deadly diseases among workers. No wonder it took 10 years to complete!

5. At the end of the Gaillard Cut, the ship enters the Pedro Miguel lock. The lock lowers the ship about 30 feet into Miraflores Lake.

6. A two-mile-long channel leads the ship to the two Miraflores locks. They lower the ship to sea level. It takes about seven minutes for water to enter or drain from the locks. The ship sails seven miles until it reaches the Pacific Ocean.

HOW Was a Bridge Built Across the Colorado River?

Engineers develop and design structures and solve problems. They are used to challenges, but this was a tough one: How to span the wide canyon between Nevada and Arizona, nearly 900 feet above the Colorado River. The answer: Build a 1,900-foot-long arch bridge.

The Mike O'Callaghan–Pat Tillman Memorial Bridge took five years to build before it opened in 2010. It is the longest and highest concrete arch bridge in the Western Hemisphere. To build it, engineers first had to measure the height and width of the canyon and the steepness of its walls. Next, they had to choose the best bridge design for the site. An arch bridge was picked because it is the best way to cross a steep canyon. The builders faced another challenge thanks to Hoover Dam, the bridge's neighbor. The engineers felt a special responsibility building a large structure next to an engineering marvel. Most people think they succeeded and produced their own engineering marvel.

The bridge has two side-by-side arches made of steel and concrete. The arches were put together in 52 pieces, half on each side of the canyon. Each piece was 24 feet long.

Each half of the arches was built over the river, and they met in the center. Dozens of temporary cables held up the arches as the bridge grew longer and longer above the river. The cables were attached to temporary towers 155 feet in height.

Longest U.S. Suspension Bridges

Many long bridges are suspension bridges. The roadway is held up by wire ropes that stretch from tall towers to the road.

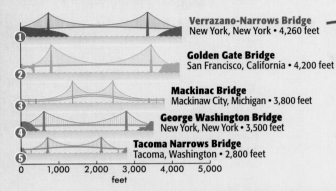

① **Verrazano-Narrows Bridge**
New York, New York • 4,260 feet

② **Golden Gate Bridge**
San Francisco, California • 4,200 feet

③ **Mackinac Bridge**
Mackinaw City, Michigan • 3,800 feet

④ **George Washington Bridge**
New York, New York • 3,500 feet

⑤ **Tacoma Narrows Bridge**
Tacoma, Washington • 2,800 feet

0   1,000   2,000   3,000   4,000   5,000
feet

The final step was to build a road deck over the arches. It is made of concrete poured over 36 steel girders, each weighing 50 tons.

Large columns are built into the rocks on either side of the river. They help hold up the roadway approaches to the bridge.

The bridge has four car lanes and a walkway that lets visitors view the river and the nearby dam. Before the bridge was built, people had to drive across the top of Hoover Dam. The new bridge allows more cars to cross the canyon much faster.

HOW to Build a Spaghetti Bridge

Modern bridges are impressive metal structures, but a bridge can be as simple as a log that falls across a stream. Over the centuries, many materials have been used to span water, valleys, or roads, including wood, ropes, and a tough plant called bamboo.

Stone bridges have been constructed for thousands of years—and they can last just as long. Hundreds of stone bridges built by the ancient Romans are still found in many countries. In the 1700s, iron was first used in a bridge. Later, concrete and steel became favorite materials of bridge builders. One material bridge builders don't use is spaghetti. But you can build a pasta bridge—just don't try to eat it!

FACTOID

The spaghetti bridge world record was set by two college students from Hungary. They built a bridge that weighed about two pounds and held a weight of 975 pounds.

What You Need

- 8 marshmallows
- 2–3 strands of uncooked linguini
- 13-14 strands of uncooked spaghetti (try to use spaghetti that's about the same diameter as the linguini)
- 1 paper clip
- 1 envelope
- Scissors
- 40 coins

What to Do

1 Use the scissors to snip off one corner of the envelope. This will be a coin basket.

2 Unbend one end of the paper clip. Poke it through the top of the envelope and bend it into a hook shape so it holds the coin basket.

3 Make two pyramids of equal size by sticking the spaghetti through the marshmallows. Each pyramid will need four marshmallows and six strands of spaghetti.

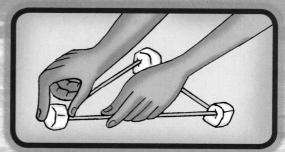

4 Stand up the two pyramids near each other so they are less than the length of a spaghetti strand apart.

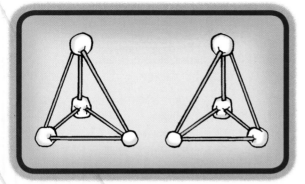

5 Connect one end of a strand of spaghetti to the marshmallow at the top of one pyramid. Connect the other end to the marshmallow atop the other pyramid.

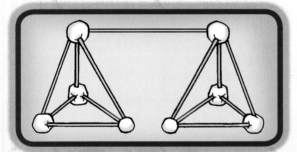

6 Hang the coin basket in the middle of the strand of spaghetti that connects the two pyramids. This is the bridge. Add coins one by one to the basket until the spaghetti breaks. Note how many coins it takes to break the bridge.

7 Connect the two pyramids with a strand of linguini. Repeat the experiment. Note the difference in the number of coins it took to make each bridge collapse.

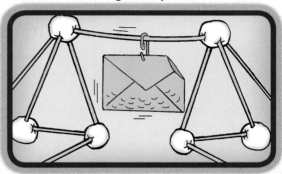

What Happened

Two strong shapes held up the bridge: triangles and circles. The spaghetti pyramids are made of triangles. Triangles are strong because they are rigid and won't bend. Spaghetti is shaped like a cylinder, and round objects have great strength. Stress is distributed equally throughout them, and they will bend in any direction. Rectangles bend in one direction. The linguini is shaped like a rectangle and so it bends and breaks.

FACTOID

Kelowna, Canada, is famous for its Spaghetti Bridge contest sponsored by Okanagan University. Each year, kids and adults compete to build the strongest bridges out of dry noodles. This spaghetti bridge, built by elementary school students, held about 77 pounds before it bent.

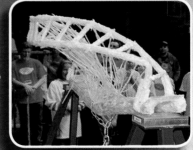

HOW to Build a Pyramid

Pyramids have fascinated builders for thousands of years. Not only does a pyramid have a cool shape, but it is also very stable. Because it has much more weight on the bottom than the top, it won't topple. That's why cheerleaders and circus acrobats enjoy making human pyramids.

The outside surfaces of a pyramid slant up to meet at a point, called the apex. A pyramid can be built with different numbers of sides. A three-sided pyramid has a triangle-shaped base, so it is called a triangular pyramid. A pyramid with four sides has a four-sided base. It is called a square pyramid. The base of the pyramid with five sides is a pentagonal, or five-sided, pyramid, and so on. It took workers 20 years to build the Great Pyramid, in Giza, Egypt. But you can build a great pyramid in less than an hour.

FACTOID

The entrance to the Louvre Museum in Paris, France, is a 70-foot-high metal and glass pyramid surrounded by three smaller pyramids.

What You Need

- Small block or other square object to use as a pattern, about two or three inches on a side. You can use a larger block to make a larger pyramid. In that case, you might also need larger papers.
- Stiff white paper, about 8½ inches by 11 inches or larger
- A piece of paper a little larger than the block
- Pen or pencil
- Scissors
- Glue
- Ruler or triangle

What to Do

1 Place the square block over the smaller paper and trace the block's four sides with the pen. You should have drawn a perfect square on the card. This square is the pattern square. Place the block in the center of the large white paper and trace it again. This is the base square.

2 Cut out the pattern square with scissors. Then fold the square in half. Open it up and fold it again the other way, so the pattern square has been folded into quarters.

3 Make a dot with the pen at each fold on the edge of the square.

4 Place the pattern square on top of the base square, so the sides line up. Use the pattern square to mark the center point of each side on the base square: The dots on the pattern card will be at the center points.

5 Take the pattern square and place one of its points on a dot on the base square. Then make a dot on the white paper at the opposite point of the pattern square. The dot should line up with the opposite center points of the pattern square. Repeat this for the remaining three dots of the base square.

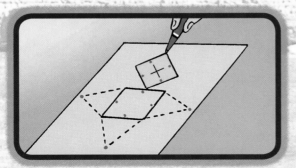

6 Draw straight lines connecting the dots on the white paper to the corners of the base square. You can use a ruler. It should end up looking like a four-pointed star, or four triangles, with a box at the center. Draw a small tab or flap on the same side of each star.

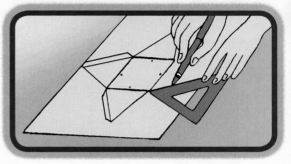

7 Use the scissors to cut along the lines of the triangles. Fold the four stars, or triangles, in toward the box, so they meet to form a pyramid. They should fit together. Unfold them. Fold and unfold the tabs.

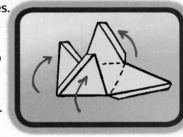

8 Glue each tab and press it against the inside of the adjoining triangle. If you have trouble sticking it to the inside of the triangles, stick it to the outside. Decorate your pyramid to make it look like an Egyptian pyramid. Or coat the pyramid in glue and sprinkle it with sand so it has a desert look.

HOW Do Scientists Uncover and Remove Fossils from a Dig?

Scientists who look for and study the life of the past are called paleontologists (pay-lee-ahn-*tah*-lo-jists). They learn about prehistoric times by digging up and studying fossils, which are the remains of ancient plants and animals. Most fossils are bones and teeth—the hardest part of an animal.

Finding fossils isn't a snap. Scientists might walk slowly for days across deserts, canyons, hills, or along riverbanks looking at rocks. They keep their eyes peeled for a slightly different color that stands out: It might be a prehistoric bone. Once scientists discover a bone, they try to figure out what kind of animal it belonged to. That's not always simple, because the fossils might be very tiny or broken. When scientists do find a fossil that interests them, the real work begins: Removing it from the rock.

Paleontologists dig out dinosaur fossils from a vertical wall in Dinosaur National Monument, located in Utah and Colorado.

To understand how crystals form, how optical illusions trick our eyes, or why you don't fall out of a roller coaster, you need to know science. Science tells us how the world works.

1

After a fossil is discovered, scientists use a pick to gently dig away a block of rock around it. They clear away the rock fragments with a brush. If the bone is easily breakable, it is covered in liquid glue to harden it.

2

As scientists cut around the fossil, they wrap both the delicate bone and the surrounding rock in a protective jacket. A jacket is made of strips of burlap drenched in plaster. The strips are layered over the fossil, then coated with more plaster.

3

After the plaster cast dries, workers lift it from the ground and carry it to a vehicle. Some casts are so heavy, trucks or even helicopters are needed to take them from the site.

4

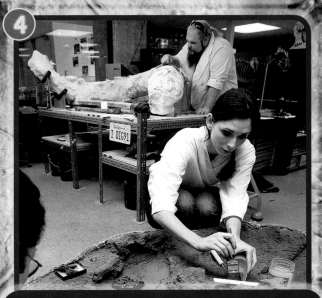

Casts are sent to a lab at a museum or university. There, researchers cut off the cast and remove rock from the bones with tools such as brushes and grinders. They clean the bones and glue back together any broken ones.

HOW Are Oil Spills Cleaned Up?

In 2010, an explosion on an oil rig in the Gulf of Mexico killed 11 workers and sent oil spewing into the water. Before the leak was plugged, 206 million gallons of oil had flowed into the Gulf, making it the worst oil spill in U.S. history. In an average year (2010 was not an average year), ships and pipelines spill about 1.3 million gallons of oil in U.S. waters.

Oil spills happen for many reasons, from natural disasters such as hurricanes and earthquakes to accidents involving tankers, pipelines, and oil storage tanks. Whatever the cause, oil spills—especially those in the ocean—harm animals and the environment. Because oil spills have become common, more and more ways of cleaning them up have been invented.

Absorbers: Sponge-like material, called sorbents, are dropped into the water to absorb oil. Sorbents can be natural like straw or sawdust, or they can be human-made materials. When they absorb all they can, the oil-soaked sponges are removed from the water.

Booms: These long, snake-like tubes float on the water like a fence to corral an oil slick and keep it from spreading.

Troubled Waters

The pipe that leaked oil in the Gulf of Mexico has been plugged. But that didn't end the problems the spill caused. The oil was very bad for birds. More than 2,000 birds covered in oil had been found alive. More than 2,000 other oily birds were found dead. People were also hurt by the oil spill. Many who live in the Gulf region make their living from the fishing industry. People lost their jobs when the oily waters were closed for fishing. Gulf towns usually packed with beach visitors were empty the summer of 2010. Hotels, restaurants, and stores lost money.

Slowly the Gulf of Mexico was restored. Wildlife were cleaned. Beaches opened. People returned to their jobs as fishers. But still, no one is sure what effect the oil spill will have on Gulf waters in the years to come.

Burning: Sometimes an oil slick is set on fire to burn off the oil. Not everyone likes this method because the smoke causes air pollution.

Other tools to clean up include:

Chemicals: These are sometimes used to break the oil into small droplets. Waves and currents break the droplets into smaller droplets.

Stickers: Chemicals called gelling agents make the oil form small, rubber-like balls. Nets or suction machines remove the balls from the water.

Germs: Some bacteria in water slowly eat oil. To speed things up, extra bacteria can be added to the water.

HOW Are Birds Cleaned After an Oil Spill?

An oil spill harms the environment, hurts businesses, and is a disaster for wildlife—especially marine animals. Oil spills affect many sea creatures, from plankton and oysters to shrimp and fish. The gloppy muck often covers a seabird's feathers, making them less waterproof. A bird soaked with oil can't stay warm, float, or swim. When the bird tries to clean itself, it swallows the oil.

Even marine animals at the top of the food chain, such as killer whales, are endangered by oil. Oil may plug up the whale's blowhole, so it can't breathe. And if a whale eats fish contaminated by oil, it will get sick. Fortunately, when oil spills take place, wildlife rescue centers rush into action. They work hard to save animals affected by the oil.

1 Birds covered in oil are captured and brought into a cleaning center.

2 Workers examine the seabird, checking its physical condition. The bird isn't thoroughly washed until it rests and after a veterinarian gives the okay. Washing a stressed or upset bird could kill it.

③

Workers first clean off a bird's eyes and breathing passages. The bird may be given a liquid to drink to help clean its insides. Then the bird is washed in a tub of warm water containing a small amount of dishwashing liquid. This bird is being gently cleaned with a toothbrush.

④

The bird gets a shower of clean water to wash away soap and oil. This is repeated several times until all the oil is removed.

Wash Up

Check out how soap and water can clean oil off a bird's feathers.

What You Need
- A feather (you can buy one at a craft store)
- Water in a spray bottle
- Vegetable oil
- Water combined with a little dishwashing liquid
- Old toothbrush

What You Do
1. Spray water on the feather. The feather repels the water.

2. Dip the feather in oil. The feather should droop slightly because it absorbs the oil.

3. Wash the feather with the soapy water. Scrub the feather with the toothbrush. Can you remove the oil?

What Happened
A bird's feathers are naturally waterproof. But they are not oil-proof. A bird covered in oil can't float, swim, or fly. Soap, such as dishwashing liquid, can remove the oil. The oil sticks to the soap and can be washed away with the water.

⑤

The clean, healthy bird is placed in a pool of warm water, where it uses its beak to preen, or smooth, its feathers. Then it is put into a pool of cold water to make sure it can float and its feathers are waterproof. After the bird gets a clean bill of health from doctors, it is released back into the wild.

HOW Do Roller Coasters Go Up and Down?

A roller coaster is like a scary movie: It gives riders thrills and chills without putting them in danger. How do these scream machines move people up, down, and around? It takes energy. As a roller coaster car is pulled up the first hill, it stores potential energy. The higher it goes, the more potential energy it has. When gravity pulls the coaster down the track, the coaster releases the potential energy. Now it has kinetic energy, which is the energy an object has when it moves. The faster an object moves, the more kinetic energy it has. The coaster is moving fastest after it goes down the first and highest hill. This gives the car enough energy to go up the next hill.

A coaster can't go up and down hills forever. Air resistance and the friction of the wheels against the track make the car lose energy and eventually slow down. That's why each hill is made smaller and smaller.

Safety bars and heavy seat belts keep riders inside the car.

Motorized chains pull the cars up the first hill. Some rides use magnets in the cars and track to pull the coaster quickly up the first hill.

The first hill is the highest. The coaster gains enough kinetic energy going down this first hill to go up the next hill. The second hill is next highest. At the bottom of the second hill, the car has just enough energy to reach the top of the third hill.

TOP 5 Highest Roller Coasters in the World

COASTER	HEIGHT (FT)	AMUSEMENT PARK	LOCATION
1. Kingda Ka	456	Six Flags Great Adventure	Jackson, New Jersey
2. Top Thrill Dragster	420	Cedar Point	Sandusky, Ohio
3. Tower of Terror II	377	Dreamworld	Coomera, Australia
4. Steel Dragon 2000	318	Nagashima Spa Land	Nagashima, Japan
5. Millennium Force	310	Cedar Point	Sandusky, Ohio

Source: Roller Coaster Data Base

Kingda Ka

Millennium Force

Tower of Terror II

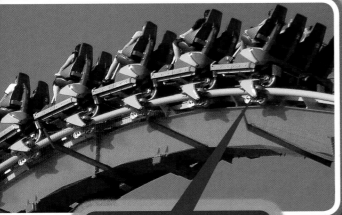

Three sets of car wheels run above, under, and alongside the track. They keep the car locked on when it makes twists, turns, and loop-de-loops.

Riders on a loop-de-loop don't fall out thanks to centrifugal (cen-*trif*-uh-gull) force. The force of the car moving in a circle pushes riders back toward the floor of the car. It's the same as when you whirl a bucket of water in a big circle around your head. The water stays in the bucket!

HOW Do Optical Illusions Trick Our Eyes?

Optical illusions are tricky. They can make you think that something is bigger or smaller than it is. They can fool you into believing that colors are brighter or darker than they are. They can hoodwink you into swearing that an object is moving when it isn't. If you think optical illusions trick your eyes, you've been tricked again! They actually fool your brain. The eyes gather information, but the brain chooses what you see. Sometimes that choice is the wrong one.

There are many types of optical illusions. Some are drawings with details left out. Your brain makes mistakes as it fills in the spaces, and you see something that isn't there. A drawing that looks three dimensional is an optical illusion. See if your brain falls for these optical illusions.

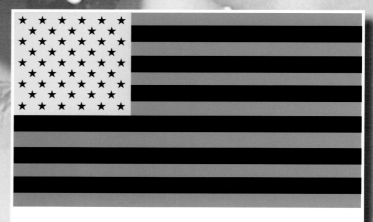

Stare at the flag for about 30 seconds. Then quickly look at the white space. You should see a red, white, and blue flag. Here's why: Sometimes when you stare at something and then look away, you continue to see the image for a moment. That's called an afterimage. The afterimage of a color picture shows up as its complementary colors. Blue-green is a complement of red. Yellow is a complement of blue, and so on. When you look at the blue stripes too long, the cells in your eyes that are sensitive to blue get tired. When you look away, the blue cells don't work, but the nearby red cells do. They send out a strong signal, and you see red stripes instead of blue.

FACTOID

A movie is an optical illusion. It is really just a series of still pictures that are projected on a screen so fast, the mind sees them as an image that moves smoothly.

Look at the two arrows. Which do you think is longer? If you measure the lines connecting the fins, you'll find that the lengths are the same.

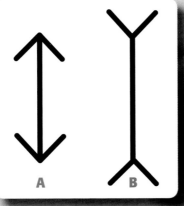

Although the lines are the same length, your brain tells you that arrow B is longer than arrow A. Scientists are not sure why this illusion works. One theory is that the fins affect the way you mentally measure the lines. Since the fins and arrow of B have more total length than the fins and arrow of A, you think arrow B is longer than arrow A.

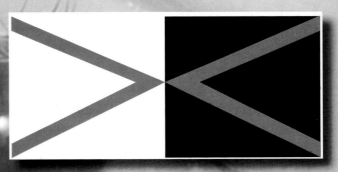

Look at the two sideway Vs. Does one look darker than the other? Actually, they are exactly the same shade of gray. One looks lighter than the other because of contrast. An object seems lighter against a dark background than it does against a light background.

Is this a picture of two faces or a vase? When you look at a picture, your brain tends to separate parts of the picture into the main object and the background. The main object always stands out more than the background. When you look at this picture, the vase is the main object if you see white as the background. If you see black as the background, the two faces are the main objects.

Are the colors in the small boxes different? On the top row, the small box on the right seems redder than the small box on the left. On the bottom row, the small box on the left seems greener than the one on the right. But in each row, the small boxes are the same color. Contrast can fool us. Colors seem to change depending on the color of the background.

HOW Is a Fireworks Show Staged?

Fourth of July isn't the same without a fireworks display. The experts who put on these shows are called pyrotechnicians (pi-roh-tek-*nish*-unz). They build and shoot off the fireworks. To create a spectacular show, pyrotechnicians must figure out what types of fireworks should go off—and in what order. They must think about the colors, sounds, heights, and patterns of fireworks. In some shows, the fireworks must go along with music. Pyrotechnicians are the only people legally allowed to handle fireworks in most states. Leave fireworks to the experts, and enjoy the show!
 Here is how a professional fireworks show is put on.

②

③

①

④

Hundreds of steel tubes, or mortars, are set up. A mortar holds a single firework, called a shell. Mortars are placed at different angles so the fireworks will explode in different areas in the sky.

A pyrotechnician places a shell in each mortar. At the bottom of the shell is gunpowder. When the powder explodes, it sends the shell into the sky.

Before the show, workers begin to connect the fireworks to a firing panel with wires. The firing panel sits far from the mortars.

It's a Blast!

An aerial firework is a firework that explodes high in the air. To build one, an expert places a fuse in a shell, or paper tube. The shell is packed with black powder, as well as chemicals formed into little balls or cubes, called stars. It's the stars that give the fireworks their colors and patterns in the sky. Finally, the shell is wrapped in thick paper hardened by paste and shaped into a cylinder or sphere.

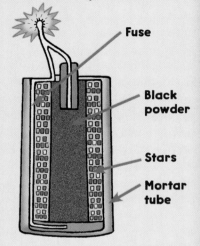

Fuse

Black powder

Stars

Mortar tube

When a firework is lit, black powder in the bottom of the shell rockets it out of a mortar and into the sky. As the firework rises, the fuse inside the shell burns down. When the shell reaches its peak, the fuse lights the black powder in the shell. The exploding powder makes the stars burn in a shower of colorful sparks.

5

The fireworks are set off far enough away from spectators so pieces of the exploding shells won't land on the crowds. At a July Fourth fireworks display in New York City, they were set off from a barge in the middle of a river.

At the press of a button, an electric current ignites the powder in a mortar. One by one, the fireworks blast 300 to 600 feet into the sky and burst into colors. The final fireworks, the "finale," is loud and spectacular. The crowds applaud.

HOW Does an Iceberg Form?

"Iceberg right ahead!" That's what a crew member of the *Titanic* cried out just before his ship hit a huge block of ice in the North Atlantic in 1912. Most icebergs, including the one that sank the *Titanic*, start off in Greenland. Every year, between 15,000 and 30,000 icebergs are calved, or break off, from glaciers in Greenland. A smaller number form in Alaska, while some of the biggest break off from Antarctic ice shelves. One Antarctic iceberg was the size of Connecticut!

Just-born bergs begin large—if it isn't at least 98 feet thick, it isn't considered an iceberg. But most melt away in a few months. Some melt down into growlers, which are icebergs that are about as big as a piano. Slightly larger ones, called bergy bits, are about the size of a small house.

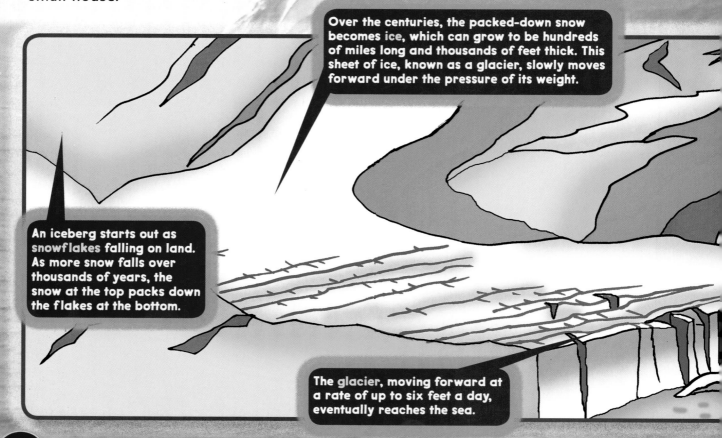

Over the centuries, the packed-down snow becomes ice, which can grow to be hundreds of miles long and thousands of feet thick. This sheet of ice, known as a glacier, slowly moves forward under the pressure of its weight.

An iceberg starts out as snowflakes falling on land. As more snow falls over thousands of years, the snow at the top packs down the flakes at the bottom.

The glacier, moving forward at a rate of up to six feet a day, eventually reaches the sea.

Cool Customers

Icebergs come in all kinds of shapes and colors. Tabular icebergs are shaped like a table, with a flat top and steep sides. Tabular icebergs are very large. Non-tabular icebergs can have a rounded top (dome iceberg), pointy parts (pinnacle berg), a slot cut through by water (dry-dock berg), or just about any other odd shape caused by melting ice.

Most icebergs are transparent. But they look white because air bubbles in the ice reflect light. An iceberg can look blue, too, because all the colors of light are absorbed by its thick ice except blue. Some icebergs are green or yellowish, which can be caused by the berg's shape and thickness, as well as from bits of rock, soil, or sea life in the ice.

Tabular iceberg

Pinnacle iceberg

Dry-dock iceberg

As the end of the glacier moves out past the land, the ice breaks off, or calves, into the sea. The chunks that fall into the water are icebergs.

Dome iceberg

Icebergs that form near Greenland are carried by ocean currents toward the North Atlantic Ocean. Most melt on the way there—only one percent of Greenland's bergs ever reach the Atlantic.

HOW to Make a Rain Forest

Lush and green, tropical rain forests grow in regions along the equator, from Africa to South and Central America to Asia. It rains often in a rain forest (duh!). In addition, plants and trees give off large amounts of water. The water turns to vapor and hangs over the canopy, or top, of the rain forest like a cloud. More than 50 percent of all animal life and about two-thirds of flowering plants on Earth live in rain forests. The largest rain forest is the Amazon, in South America. Here, a four-square-mile area may contain 750 species of trees, 125 kinds of mammals, 400 types of birds, and 100 kinds of reptiles.

Rain forests are amazing places. If you can't travel to one, build your own. You can create a rain forest in a terrarium, which is a miniature world that grows under glass.

FACTOID

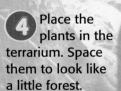

About one-half of Earth's rain forests have been cut down or burned for farmland. Rain forests once covered about 14 percent of the planet, but now only grow over 6 percent of land.

What You Need

- Large glass jar and lid
- Gravel or tiny pebbles
- Small plants
- Soil
- Small shovel
- Paper cup
- Water

What to Do

1 Look for plants in open fields, woods, and backyards. (Make sure first that you're allowed to dig them up.) When you dig up plants, get as much of the root as possible. Bring the plants home in paper cups and keep the roots wet. If you can't dig up plants, buy several small ones, such as wintergreen, boxwood, ferns, peperomia, philodendron, spider plants, and mosses.

2 Wash and dry the glass container.

3 Put gravel or pebbles at the bottom of the container.

4 Place the plants in the terrarium. Space them to look like a little forest.

5 Add soil deep enough to cover plant roots.

6 Carefully water the terrarium. The soil should be damp, but not soggy.

7 Cover the jar with the lid so no air leaks out.

8 Put your terrarium in a place with lots of light, but not direct sunlight. You don't have to water your rain forest often. This forest makes its own rain.

What Happened

The plants stay alive in the closed jar because they use the same air again and again. In daylight, plants breathe in carbon dioxide and give off oxygen. At night, they change oxygen back into carbon dioxide. Water is also recycled. Plants drink up water from the soil and later give off water vapor through their leaves. The water vapor turns into water droplets on the sides of the jar. The water drips down back into the soil.

Riches from the Forest

Rain forests are Earth's treasure chests, and one of their most precious prizes is oxygen. Rain forests absorb carbon dioxide, a greenhouse gas, and breathe out life-giving oxygen. The rain forests give us other goodies. About one-quarter of prescription medicines in the U.S. are made from chemicals in tropical rain forest plants, including quinine, which fights malaria, muscle relaxers used in surgery, and drugs to battle cancer. Scientists continue to search for more life-saving plants in the rain forests.

Many foods that fill our supermarkets are native to the rain forest. Bananas, pineapples, oranges, peppers, lemons, coconuts, and other tasty, nutritious treats grow in rain forests. So do coffee beans, cashews, vanilla, and cacao seeds, which are used to make chocolate. Rain forests provide us with burlap for bags, rope for nets, fibers for stuffing pillows and life jackets. They give us oils for perfumes and even wax that keeps M&Ms from melting in your hands.

FACTOID

The world's largest fossilized rain forest was discovered in Georgetown, Illinois. The 300-million-year-old forest covers 15 square miles. It contains fossils of trees (shown right), mosses, shrubs, and ferns as tall as 12 feet.

HOW to Grow Crystals

What do diamonds, table salt, and sugar have in common? They're all crystals. Crystals are formed by atoms or molecules that are arranged in repeating patterns. When new atoms get attached to a crystal, they keep adding to the same pattern. Different crystals have different-shaped patterns. If you look under a powerful microscope, you'd see that many diamond crystals are in the shape of triangular prisms. Salt crystals are tiny cubes, and sugar crystals are oblong and slanted at the ends.

Crystals aren't alive but they can grow. If the molecules of the same type of crystal come in contact with each other, they often connect to form larger crystals. This happens in underground caves, where crystals grow to dozens of feet long. Nature takes years to form some crystals, but you can grow them a lot faster in your home.

What You Need

- 1 to 3 cups of sugar
- One-half cup of salt
- Water
- A spoon
- A small pot
- 2 glasses
- 2 pencils
- 2 paper clips
- Two pieces of string or thread, about 5 inches long each
- Tape
- Measuring cup

What to Do

1 Tie one piece of string to one end of each paper clip.

2 Tape the other end of each string to the middle of each pencil. Set aside.

3 Boil a cup of water. Carefully remove the pot from the heat (have an adult help you). Stir in sugar a few teaspoons at a time, until no more can dissolve.

4 Pour the sugar water into one of the glasses.

5 Place the pencil flat on top of the glass so the string dangles in the sugar water. The paper clip will keep the string steady. Don't move the glass.

6 In the other glass, repeat steps 3, 4, and 5 using table salt instead of sugar. (The salt water will be more cloudy than the sugar water).

7 After two or three weeks, you should see sugar and salt crystals forming around the string and clip in each glass.

The sugar crystals might take longer to form than the salt.

Hard Choices

Crystals are a form of mineral. A mineral is a solid substance formed underground from heat and pressure. Gold is a mineral, and so is aluminum. Scientists have discovered about 3,000 different minerals. One scientist, Friederich Mohs, drew up a list of 10 common minerals and ranked them in their order of hardness. Ten is the hardest and one is the softest. This list, called the Mohs scale, is used to compare the hardness of different substances. For example, a fingernail has a rating of 2.5 on the scale and window glass is 5.5.

1. Talc
2. Gypsum
3. Calcite
4. Flourite
5. Apatite
6. Orthoclase feldspar
7. Quartz
8. Topaz
9. Corundum
10. Diamond

What Happened

When loads of sugar (or salt) are dissolved in water, the solution becomes saturated. The water is so filled with sugar that it can't hold any more. Hot water holds more sugar than cold water does. As the glass of sugar or salt solution sits, the water cools down and evaporates. The solution can hold less sugar, and so must get rid of all the extra sugar particles. When that happens, the sugar particles stick to the string in the glass. Each little particle is a pretty crystal. The same process happens with salt particles in the solution.

HOW Do Submarines Work?

Submarines do one thing that regular ships don't want to do: They sink. A sub has an outside hull and an inside hull. Between the two hulls are compartments called ballast tanks. When the tanks are filled with seawater, the sub is heavier than water. It sinks. When air is pumped into the ballast tanks to force out all the water, the sub is lighter than water. It rises.

Subs have been used to explore the depths of the oceans. They are also big weapons of war. Submarines played a major part in World War I and World War II. Today, nuclear-powered submarines packed with missiles patrol the seas. Subs are an amazing form of transportation—if you don't mind being in a tight squeeze.

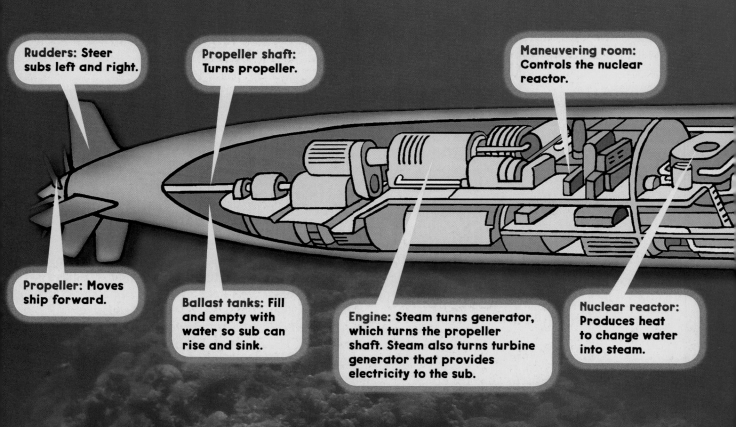

Rudders: Steer subs left and right.

Propeller shaft: Turns propeller.

Maneuvering room: Controls the nuclear reactor.

Propeller: Moves ship forward.

Ballast tanks: Fill and empty with water so sub can rise and sink.

Engine: Steam turns generator, which turns the propeller shaft. Steam also turns turbine generator that provides electricity to the sub.

Nuclear reactor: Produces heat to change water into steam.

Cars, trains, and planes make it a snap to travel just about anywhere. And new technologies promise that we'll be getting around faster and more efficiently than ever before.

FACTOID

The world's first nuclear-powered submarine, the USS *Nautilus*, was named after a submarine in the novel *20,000 Leagues Under the Sea*, by Jules Verne.

Bridge: Holds periscope, radio antennas, radar, and other electronic sensors.

Sonar room: Sonar bounces sounds off objects outside the sub. The echoes let the crew stationed here know what's out there—friends or enemies—and how far away they are.

Torpedoes and torpedo tubes

Control room and attack center: Contains systems and crew to steer ship. The orders to launch torpedoes and missiles are delivered from here.

Officers' cabin: Officers sleep here.

Sonar dome: Contains hundreds of sound detectors.

Crew bunks: Crew sleeps here.

Crew's mess: Dining room

HOW Does a Hybrid Car Work?

The United States is a nation of automobiles. In fact, there are about 245 million of them on American roads. But cars have two big problems: They cause pollution and they run on costly gas. One solution that carmakers have come up with is the hybrid car. A hybrid car is a combination of two power sources—gas and electricity.

Hybrid cars save on fuel. One reason is that they run mostly on electricity provided by batteries. And because hybrids usually are smaller and lighter than normal cars, they need less power to run. Hybrid cars are not as polluting as gas guzzlers. Electricity doesn't give off any pollution, and hybrids burn less gas and do it more efficiently than regular cars.

The batteries store electricity, which makes the electric motor run.

An electric motor powers the car. The motor also works as a generator to recharge the batteries.

The gas tank stores fuel that runs the gas engine. The tank holds less gas than those in regular cars.

The power electronics control how much electricity is used to run the car—and when to use it.

Many hybrid cars use special tires that are inflated more than usual. This causes less friction and saves on fuel.

The gas-powered engine runs the car at higher speeds or when the battery needs to be recharged. While this engine runs, it turns the generator.

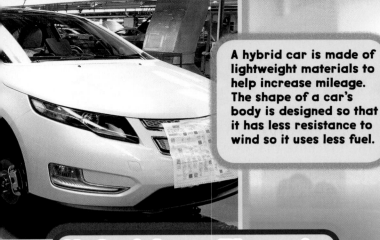

A hybrid car is made of lightweight materials to help increase mileage. The shape of a car's body is designed so that it has less resistance to wind so it uses less fuel.

A High-Flying Car

The Terrafugia Transition is a really unusual hybrid. The amazing vehicle is both a car and an airplane. The $200,000 personal aircraft gets 35 miles per gallon on the road and comes with an airbag and a parachute. On the ground, its wings are folded up. When the wings come down at an airport, it can fly two passengers about 500 miles at a speed of 105 miles per hour. With this vehicle, you need both a driver's and a pilot's license.

Hybrid vs. Electric

A hybrid car runs on both an electric motor and a gas-powered motor. The hybrid uses the electric motor to travel at slow speeds. When the car goes at higher speeds, the gas engine turns on automatically. If more power is needed, the electric motor and gas motor can work at the same time. If the batteries run low, the gas engine will take over and recharge the batteries as the car runs.

An electric car is powered only by electricity. It needs more batteries than a hybrid, often 12 to 24 of them. The batteries must be recharged about every 100 miles. They can be recharged by plugging them in at home in a wall outlet for a few hours. Charging stations, like the one in the photo below, also provide electricity for recharging batteries.

HOW Are Tunnels Dug?

Tunnels can be dug through miles of mountains or under cities. Mammoth-size machinery is used to dig the huge holes. The machine that most large projects use is called a tunnel-boring machine (TBM). It has a giant spinning disc that cuts through solid rock. TBMs were used to cut through mountains in the Alps to create the longest tunnel ever built—the Gotthard Base Tunnel that links Switzerland and Italy in Europe. The train tunnel is slightly more than 35 miles long!

1. The front of some TBMs have shields to keep pieces of rock from falling down and burying the machine.

Sometimes when transportation tunnels are dug, two tunnels are built side by side so cars or trains can travel in both directions. Most tunnels are dug from the opposite ends and meet in the middle.

The TBMs for the Gotthard tunnel each weighed about 6 million pounds and were 1,300 feet long. They dug 96 feet of tunnel a week. It takes 20 to 25 people to operate a TBM.

Longest Railroad Tunnels

TUNNEL	LOCATION	LENGTH IN MILES	OPENED
1. Gotthard Base	Switzerland-Italy	35.4	Completed 2010. Not open until 2017
2. Seikan	Japan	33.5	1988
3. Channel	England-France	31.1	1994
4. Lotschberg Base	Switzerland	21.5	2007
5. Guadarrama	Spain	17.6	2007

Source: World Book

How a Tunnel Is Built

5. An elevator carries dug-up rock to the surface. The rock might be placed in a landfill or used in another project, such as a road. At Gotthard, some rock was used to make the concrete that covered the tunnel walls.

3. Crumbled rock is carried to the back of the TBM by a conveyor belt. The rock drops into a cart and is removed from the area.

Surface

Concrete sections to line the tunnel are lowered down a shaft.

2. The rotating cutters of the TBM can be 50 feet in diameter. Their super-strong titanium teeth rotate slowly, breaking up the rock as the TBM moves forward.

4. The walls of a finished tunnel are usually lined with steel or concrete or a combination of both materials. The Gotthard tunnel walls are made of concrete and a special steel that won't break under the great pressure of the Alps.

FACTOID
Enough material was removed from the Gotthard Base Tunnel to fill the Empire State Building 13 times.

HOW Does a Maglev Train Work?

A levitating train floats in the air—but it's not a magic trick. Maglev is short for magnetic levitation, and maglev trains use the push and pull of magnetism to travel above the tracks. The opposite poles of a magnet attract each other. That attraction allows one kind of maglev train to levitate. The same poles of a magnet repel each other, which is why another kind of maglev train can float. With no friction from wheels to slow them down, these magnetic marvels can reach speeds of more than 300 miles per hour. Even the fastest American trains don't go faster than 80 miles per hour.

Today, maglev trains are running full-time only in China. But maglev trains are being tested in Germany and Japan. They may one day come to the United States. When that happens, people who love riding trains will really be floating on air!

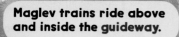

Maglev trains ride above and inside the guideway.

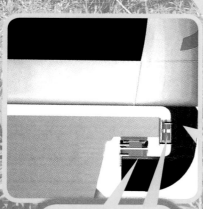

The bottom of the train contains powerful magnets.

TOP **Fastest Trains**

The fastest trains normally go at speeds of around 200 miles per hour. But some can travel much faster. These are the top speeds reached by passenger trains during test runs.

TRAIN	COUNTRY	TYPE OF TRAIN	SPEED (MILES PER HOUR)	DATE
1. JP-Maglev	Japan	maglev	361	2003
2. TGV	France	standard	357	2007
3. Shinkansen MLX01	Japan	maglev	320	1990
4. Shanghai Transrapid	China	maglev	311	2003
5. TR-07	Germany	maglev	270	1989

Source: Forbes.com/Zimbio.com

JP-Maglev

Shanghai Transrapid

Electricity sent through wires in the guideway creates an electromagnetic field. The magnetism attracts or repels the maglev's magnets (depending on the type of train), lifting the cars as much as three inches.

One type of maglev train lifts up before it moves forward and doesn't ride on the tracks. The other type rides on wheels at low speeds until the magnetism is strong enough to make it float.

Current in coils along the guideway constantly changes direction, reversing its magnetic field. The magnetism pulls the front of the train and pushes the back of the train. This makes the train go forward.

HOW to Make a Baking-Soda Boat

When submarines and other seagoing craft move forward in the water, they're applying a law discovered by the famous scientist Sir Isaac Newton. His third law of motion states that for every action there is an equal and opposite reaction. In other words, if you push an object in one direction, a force pushes you in the opposite direction. With engine-powered ships, the push comes from a propeller.

A propeller pushes water backward and the opposite reaction moves the ship forward. You don't need propellers to push water backward. Rowers do it using oars. Swimmers do it with their arms. You can apply Newton's third law of motion yourself by making a boat fueled with baking soda and vinegar.

What You Need

- A wading pool or bathtub filled with water
- Vinegar
- Baking soda
- Toilet paper
- 12-ounce plastic soda bottle with cap
- Thumbtack or push pin (optional)
- Measuring spoon and measuring cup
- A few marbles or pebbles

What to Do

1. Wash out the soda bottle so it's clean and dry inside.

2. Lay out four squares of connected toilet paper so they're flat. Fold the toilet paper in half.

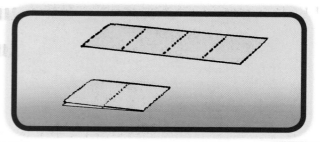

3. Put one or two tablespoons of baking soda on the two connected toilet paper squares and spread out the powder. Then roll up the toilet paper tightly so the baking soda can't leak out. You can twist the ends of the toilet paper to close them.

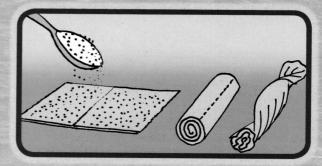

4 Add some marbles or pebbles to the bottle so it will sink partway down in the water. Place the rolled-up toilet paper in the soda bottle.

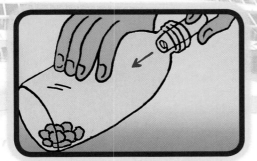

5 If you have a thumbtack or push pin use it to make several small holes in the cap. Keep the soda bottle cap handy. Or have a friend hold it. Pour one-quarter cup of vinegar into the bottle.

6 If you made holes in the cap, screw it on the bottle quickly and tightly. If you didn't make holes, place the cap on the bottle loosely, giving it only one twist.

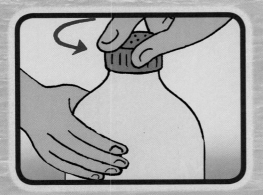

7 Shake the bottle to mix the vinegar and baking soda. Place the bottle in the pool or bathtub. Anchors aweigh!

What Happened

The boat is powered by a gas you can't see. When the baking soda and vinegar combine, they form carbon dioxide. The gas fills the bottle and escapes through the openings in the cap. The gas pushes against the water, causing the boat to move forward. Newton's third law works every time!

FACTOID

The *Oasis of the Seas*, 1,181 feet long and 236 feet wide, is the largest passenger ship in the world. The most expensive commercial ship ever constructed, it can carry more than 5,400 passengers.

HOW to Make a Paper Airplane

People have been making objects out of paper for centuries in China, Germany, Spain, and other countries. In Japan, the art of folding paper is called origami (or-eh-*gahm*-ee). Origami experts can make almost anything out of a piece of paper—from a hang glider to a beetle to a racing car. Here's how you can fold a sheet of paper into an airplane that flies. It's an uplifting experience.

FACTOIDS

● In 2004, NASA's X-43A set the speed record as the fastest ever jet-powered aircraft. For 10 seconds, the unpiloted test craft traveled at Mach 9.6, or more than nine times the speed of sound. That's 7,000 miles per hour!

● Takuo Toda, an engineer and chairman of the Japan Origami Airplane Association, says the best way to keep a paper airplane aloft is to throw it straight up in the air.

What You Need

● A sheet of paper 8½ inches by 11 inches. The paper can be smaller or bigger, but it should be rectangular.

What to Do

1 Take a sheet of paper and fold it in half the long way. Then open the paper so there is a crease down the middle.

2 Take one end of the paper and fold in one of the two corners. The inside of the corner fold should line up with the center crease. Do the same with the other corner.

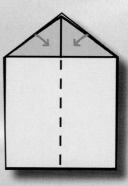

3 Fold each outer corner so it lines up with the center crease.

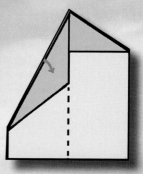

4 Fold along the main crease so you can see the body of the airplane.

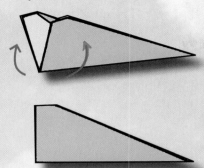

5 Fold one wing down so its edge lines up with the center crease. Repeat with the other wing.

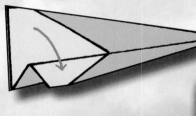

6 Unfold the wings so your plane is ready for takeoff. Throw it like a dart to make it fly. If it crashes too quickly, adjust the wings.

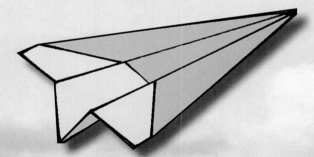

Strangest Airplanes

Check out these weird aircraft. They are just "plane" crazy!

1. VZ-9AV Avrocar It looks like a flying saucer or a giant hub cap. Its biggest problem? Anytime it flew higher than 3 feet, it wobbled like Jell-O.

2. H-4 Hercules (Spruce Goose) At 320 feet from the tip of one wing to the tip of the other, the Spruce Goose's wingspan was longer than a football field. Its body was made of laminated wood glued together.

3. Martin Marietta X-24 Something seems missing from this little jet—its wings! The Air Force built it to test how a spacecraft might act when reentering Earth's atmosphere. Even wingless, the plane went 1,036 miles per hour.

4. Vought V-173 (Flying Pancake) This flat plane was made of wood and fabric—and no, it didn't run on syrup. The plane just didn't stack up, so now it sits in the Smithsonian Institution's Air and Space Museum.

5. Zveno Bomber Fighter This plane was double trouble! In the 1920's, the Soviet Air Force built a giant bomber that carried small fighter planes attached to the wings above and below the main body of the bomber. If the "mother ship" was attacked, the fighters would launch like angry bees to protect it.

Chapter 7 Home Tech

HOW Does a Microwave Oven Cook Food?

There's fast food. And then there's faster food. A microwave oven can heat up some foods in a minute or less.

A microwave oven cooks with a type of radiation called microwaves, which are similar to the waves that transmit TV. Microwaves don't heat air. Instead, they penetrate food, making the food's water and fat molecules vibrate. The vibrations produce heat in a jiffy. Microwaves don't heat up plastic, ceramics, paper, or glass. So, food in a microwave often sits on plates made of these materials. When you pull out a cool plate from a microwave, it can fool you into thinking the food isn't hot. But it is—so be careful before you take a bite!

Microwaves cause water to vibrate in the food more than two billion times a second. This vibration causes friction, which produces energy in the form of heat. Foods won't cook unless they are in—or contain—some water.

A turntable spins so the microwaves reach all parts of the food.

Your home has plenty of incredible inventions that you probably take for granted. In this chapter, you'll discover many machines that make our lives easier.

Microwaves bounce off a kind of fan called a stirrer. This scatters the microwaves throughout the oven. The microwaves bounce around until they enter the food.

Electricity passes through a tube called a magnetron, which produces microwaves. This energy is aimed at the stirrer.

Microwave Man!

Percy Spencer is the father of fast food. In 1946, Spencer was testing a device called a **magnetron** in a lab when he discovered something strange. A candy bar in his pocket had melted. Spencer put some unpopped popcorn near the magnetron. Pretty soon, the popcorn started popping. Spencer realized that microwaves produced by the magnetron could cook food. Spencer and the company he worked for eventually built a microwave oven. It was more than five feet high and two feet wide and weighed 670 pounds. The huge oven was used in commercial kitchens. It wasn't until about 20 years later that a smaller, home version of the microwave oven was introduced. It soon became a popular cooking tool in people's kitchens.

FACTOID

Microwaves can penetrate pizza, but not the door of a microwave oven. The door is covered by a metal mesh that blocks the microwaves. The holes in the mesh are big enough to see through but too small for microwaves to pass through.

HOW Does a Lock Work?

There are locks for bikes, locks for bank vaults, locks for doors and windows, locks for diaries, and locks for lockers. Just about everyone keeps valuables under lock and key. And people have been doing that since the time of the ancient Egyptians, who made large wooden locks and keys about 4,000 years ago. The ancient Romans and Chinese weren't very trusting either. They built simple locks from metal.

Locks didn't change much until the end of the 1700s, when a few Englishmen began to make more secure devices. Today, a variety of locks keeps items safe, from combination locks with numbered dials, to vaults that use timing devices, to locks that operate with magnetic keys.

One of the most common locks used today is a cylinder with pins inside. To open it, the pins are lifted by a key with the right shape. This is called a pin and tumbler lock.

A Pin and Tumbler Lock

1

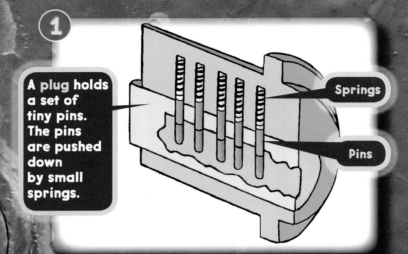

A plug holds a set of tiny pins. The pins are pushed down by small springs.

Springs

Pins

3

2

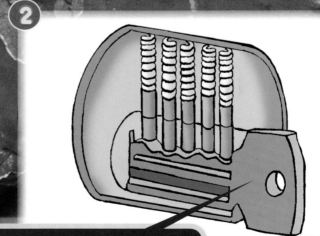

The pins prevent the plug from turning. The key slides into the plug. If the key has edges with the correct shape, it will push up the pins until they are out of the way.

Lock and Roll

Now the key can turn the plug. A key with the wrong-shaped edges won't lift all the pins out of the way, and the key won't turn.

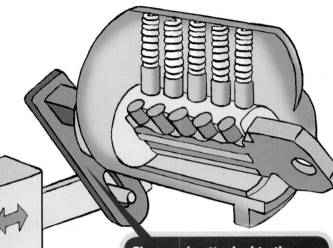

The cam is attached to the bolt, which is fixed to the door. When the plug turns, the cam turns as well, pulling the bolt.

When the bolt is turned by the cam, it unlocks the door.

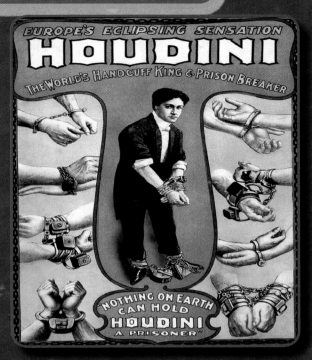

EUROPE'S ECLIPSING SENSATION
HOUDINI
THE WORLD'S HANDCUFF KING & PRISON BREAKER

"NOTHING ON EARTH CAN HOLD HOUDINI A PRISONER"

FACTOID

In 1948, Linus Yale Sr. patented a pin tumbler lock that fit in a cylinder. His son, Linus Jr. improved the lock, which today is called a Yale lock.

Not many locks could hold **Harry Houdini**, who lived from 1874 to 1926. The world's most famous escape artist, Houdini would let himself be locked up in ways that seemed impossible to get out of. Yet he always escaped. In the early 1900s, Houdini challenged police in many cities to chain and handcuff him, and lock him in the local jail cell. Each time, Houdini escaped. He also escaped from many hair-raising situations, such as a locked crate thrown into a river and a locked glass container filled with water.

How did he do it? Houdini knew how to pick, or open, just about any type of lock. He was able to open handcuffs by banging them against something hard. He knew how to open a lock with a shoestring. Houdini also cheated: He hid tools for opening locks, as well as keys. When he couldn't hide a key, he swallowed it and brought it up when no one was looking. If his hands were bound, he could turn the key with his teeth!

HOW Does a Toilet Flush Away Waste?

Getting rid of poop can be a problem. The earliest form of waste disposal was a pit in the ground. In ancient India, some cities had toilets that drained waste into underground chambers. The toilets of early Romans dropped waste into running water that carried it away. In Europe during the Middle Ages, many people deposited their waste in bowls, called chamber pots. People sometimes threw the contents of the pots out the window and into the street, where it flowed into open drains.

It wasn't until 1596 that the first flush toilet was invented, by Englishman Sir John Harrington. Over the following centuries, advances were made in toilet technology— as well as in toilet-related products. For example, in 1857, Joseph Gayetty came up with the idea of selling toilet paper in a package. The Scott Paper Company started selling toilet paper on a roll in 1879.

By the early 1900s, the modern toilet had been developed, and today it may be the most important seat in the house.

FACTOID

The most expensive toilet on Earth isn't on Earth. It's the one used by astronauts on the International Space Station. Each toilet costs $19 million.

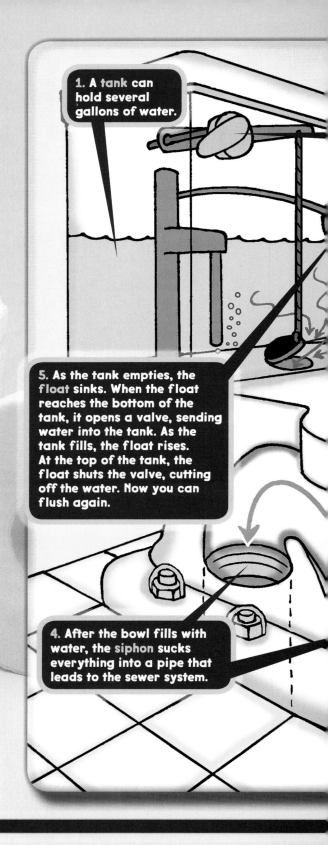

1. A tank can hold several gallons of water.

5. As the tank empties, the float sinks. When the float reaches the bottom of the tank, it opens a valve, sending water into the tank. As the tank fills, the float rises. At the top of the tank, the float shuts the valve, cutting off the water. Now you can flush again.

4. After the bowl fills with water, the siphon sucks everything into a pipe that leads to the sewer system.

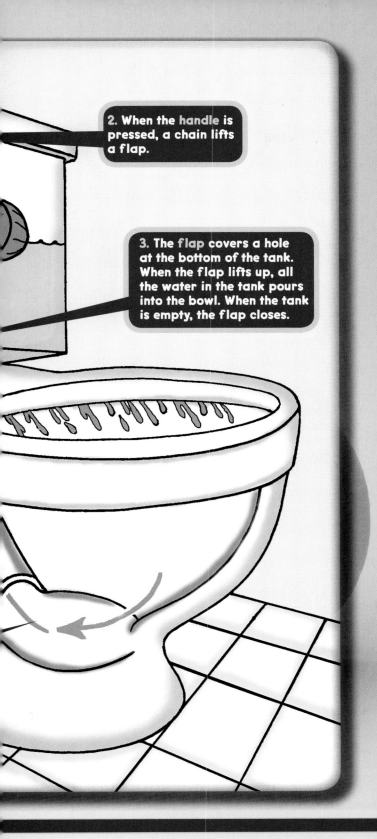

2. When the handle is pressed, a chain lifts a flap.

3. The flap covers a hole at the bottom of the tank. When the flap lifts up, all the water in the tank pours into the bowl. When the tank is empty, the flap closes.

Waste Not...

Most toilets whoosh down several gallons of water every time they flush. Toilets account for 25 percent of all water used in a house. To save water, new types of toilets have been invented.

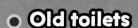

○ Old toilets

use between 3 and 5 gallons a flush. Newer toilets are able to flush while only using 1.6 gallons. That can save the average home 100 gallons a day.

○ Dual flush toilets

allow users to flush two different ways. Press one button for solid waste and the toilet uses 1.6 gallons. For liquid waste, it flushes 0.79 gallons.

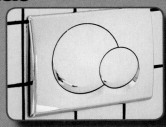

○ Composting toilets

use almost no water. The waste goes into a container that changes it into useable compost. Compost is made when bacteria break down natural substances. Owners of a composting toilet might have to add air, worms, or bacteria to the container to help the waste become safe compost. Fans remove any smells in the bathroom through a pipe that leads outside.

FACTOID

Among the many names for toilet are latrine, water closet, privy, lavatory, throne, chamber pot, commode, and john.

HOW Does a Zipper Zip?

How could we live without zippers? Well, people managed to survive without them for thousands of years. In ancient times, people held together their animal-hide clothes with pins made of thorns. Later civilizations, such as the Greeks and Egyptians, kept clothes from opening with metal pins, clasps, or cloth ties. A major fastener advance came in the Middle Ages with the invention of the button (and the buttonhole, of course). In the 1800s, two more improvements were introduced: safety pins and snaps.

The big fastener breakthrough came from Gideon Sundback. He invented the modern zipper in 1913. Still, this fastener didn't catch on until the 1930s, when it got the name "zipper." Suddenly, zippers were sewn onto just about anything that opened and closed, from dresses to rubber boots. Is the zipper an important invention? Look in your closet: It's an open and shut case!

A zipper has two tracks.

Each track holds a row of teeth. The teeth on one track mesh with those on the other track.

The slider opens and closes the zipper. Inside the slider are little wedges. When zipping closed, the wedges lock the hooks into the hollows. When zipping open, the wedges pop the hooks off the hollows.

FACTOID

The word "zipper" is an example of onomatopoeia (on-oh-*mah*-toh-pee-ah). This means giving a word a name that imitates the sound the word is associated with. Zipper sounds like the noise a zipper makes. A few other such words are splat, buzz, snort, honk, tinkle, beep, crash, sizzle, slurp, and whir. Can you think of other examples of onomatopoeia?

Fasten-ating Invention

Instead of zippers, some clothes and other items are fastened with Velcro, which is the brainchild of Swiss engineer Georges de Mestral. In 1941, after taking his dogs out for a walk in the woods, he noticed burrs sticking to the animals' fur. De Mestral thought those clingy seed pods from the burdock plant might have a use.

After eight years of testing, he invented a fastener based on the burr. It came in two parts: a cotton strip covered with tiny hooks that stuck to another cotton strip covered with tiny loops. He called his invention Velcro, a combination of the words "velvet" and "crochet" (croh-shea). (Crochet is a kind of knitting.) Later, nylon replaced cotton, and Velcro became the new zipper.

Today this hook and loop fastener is used on everything from hospital gowns, airplane seat cushions, and diapers to car floor mats, carpets, and blood pressure cuffs that go around your arm. NASA attaches Velcro to objects to keep them from floating around in space. Velcro is a perfect invention except for one thing…that ripping sound!

> On one side of each tooth is a small dimple called a hollow.

> A pull tab moves the slider up and down.

> On the other side of each tooth is a bump called a hook. The hooks of one track of teeth lock into the hollows of the other track of teeth.

FACTOID

Some Velcro is so strong that a five-inch-square strip can hold a one-ton load.

HOW Does a Refrigerator Keep Food Cold?

Food needs to chill out. When the temperature is above 40°F, bacteria can grow in food and spoil it. Refrigerators cool things down so food won't go bad. What did people do before there were fridges like the ones we have? They packed food in snow and ice, put it underwater, or placed it in cool cellars.

Today, cooling is more complicated. Inside a refrigerator are pipes filled with a fluid called a refrigerant. As this chemical passes through the pipes, it changes from a liquid to a gas and back to a liquid, over and over. The refrigerant becomes a gas at very low temperatures. As the liquid refrigerant circulates through the inside of the fridge, heat makes the liquid evaporate, or turn into gas. As the gas absorbs more and more heat, everything in the fridge—including food—gets cold. This happens when you sweat on a warm day. As the sweat evaporates, your skin chills. Cool!

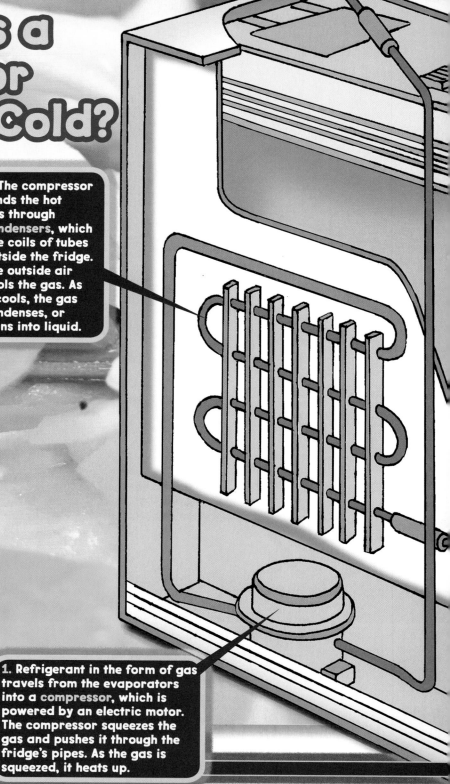

2. The compressor sends the hot gas through condensers, which are coils of tubes outside the fridge. The outside air cools the gas. As it cools, the gas condenses, or turns into liquid.

1. Refrigerant in the form of gas travels from the evaporators into a compressor, which is powered by an electric motor. The compressor squeezes the gas and pushes it through the fridge's pipes. As the gas is squeezed, it heats up.

4. A series of tubes called **evaporators** fills with the cold gas. The gas absorbs heat from everything in the fridge, which causes the fridge to chill down. The gas gets sucked into the compressor—and the cycle starts again.

Chillin'

Most freezers in home refrigerators go down to 0°F, which keeps ice cream nice and firm. But there are colder places than that. Check out the lowest of the low...temperatures.

○ On an average day, the temperature in the **Arctic** is about -30°F. The coldest temperature recorded in the Arctic was -89°F.

○ **Antarctica** is the world's coldest place, with winter temperatures reaching -94°F. Here, the coldest temperature ever on Earth was recorded: -128.6°F.

3. The liquid is pushed through a little hole called an **expansion valve**. When it passes through the hole, the liquid becomes a very cold gas.

○ One of the coldest places in the universe is inside a **cosmic cloud**. These clouds of gas and dust are far from stars, and any radiation that reaches them is blocked by dust. The temperature inside one might be as cold as -425°F.

○ The coldest anything in the universe can get is -460°F. That's called **absolute zero**.

FACTOID

Fred Wolf invented the first fridge that came with an ice tray built inside in 1913. The first metal ice tray that ejected ice cubes was invented in 1933 by Guy Tinkham.

HOW Can a Virus Make Your Computer Sick?

Just like people, computers can get sick from viruses. Computer viruses work like viruses that infect humans. They spread from computer to computer by making copies of themselves. Once inside a computer, a virus can do harm, such as making the computer run slowly or crash often, or by erasing the hard drive. Computer viruses are made and sent out by people who want to make trouble.

Computer viruses first began appearing in the late 1980s. That's when the personal computer boom began. Computer users started downloading programs and exchanging floppy disks. That made the spread of viruses simple. Today, there are "cures" for computer viruses, and so virus creators must constantly find new ways to infect computers. So it's important for computer users to know the cause and symptoms of computer viruses.

Software Virus: This is a small bit of software that gets into a computer and secretly attaches itself to other programs. Every time a user opens a program, the virus also opens and starts to run. It can reproduce itself by latching onto other programs. The virus program interferes with the workings of the computer, damages files, or causes annoying messages to appear on the screen. But it can't hurt hardware—the inner workings of the computer.

Trojan Virus: In Greek mythology, soldiers hid inside a giant wooden horse. When the horse was brought into the city of Troy, the soldiers got out and attacked. In the same way, a Trojan virus will pretend to be a music, video, or some other program. But when the program is downloaded, the virus attacks the computer. These viruses can erase a hard drive, force the computer to show ads, or allow a hacker to gain partial control of your computer.

muary 10, 2011 6:59:26 AM P

ttachment, 3.5 MB (Save

E-Mail Virus: This type of virus is sent in e-mails, usually as an attachment. Some viruses will infect a computer even if the e-mail or preview panel are simply viewed. Once opened, the virus will mail itself to all the people in the e-mail address book. Those people in turn might spread the virus to others, and so on.

WORM SPAM TROJANHRSE SPYWARE

Worm: This software program can copy itself from one computer to another without attaching itself to other programs. Worms can avoid security blocks and quickly spread from one computer to every computer in a network, such as a company or government organization. Worms also spread through e-mail address books. Worms can destroy files, and slow down or stop programs from working.

Safe Surfing

The Internet is a great tool, but it has its downsides. Protect yourself from becoming a cyber-victim by following these tips.

○ Talk with a parent about when and how you will use the Internet and send e-mails.

○ Never give out personal information online, such as your last name, home address, school, phone number, photos, where you hang out, or people you know without a parent's okay.

○ Don't share your password for your e-mail, social networking sites, or websites with anyone except your parent.

○ Never agree to meet someone in person you only met online without your parent's permission, and without a parent going with you to the meeting.

○ Get your parent's permission before signing up for a website.

○ Always discuss with your parent what websites you visit.

○ Don't be rude or a bully on the Internet. Treat everyone the way you want to be treated.

HOW Does Wi-Fi Connect to the Internet?

A hot spot sounds like a place to avoid. But not if you're a Wi-Fi user. Hotspots are areas where a computer can connect to the Internet without being plugged in to electrical, telephone, or cable lines. Wi-Fi, which stands for wireless fidelity, uses microwave signals to link computers to other computers or websites. Wi-Fi works almost anywhere. It lets a person go online while moving from room to room. Users can also connect to the Internet in a coffee shop, library, schoolroom, hotel, airport, or even in an airplane thousands of feet in the air. On a plane, the Wi-Fi signal is sent to a satellite, which beams it to Earth.

Almost all new laptops and many new desktop computers are set up for wireless use. If a computer doesn't come with wireless, a wireless adapter can be added to it. It may also need a special software program to connect to a wireless network.

To connect to the Internet, an adapter in the computer changes digital data into a radio signal. The radio signal is similar to those used to broadcast radio and TV shows. An antenna inside the computer transmits the radio signal to a device called a router.

A router is an electronic device that contains an antenna, which receives the signal sent by the computer. To work best, a router is placed near a computer and away from objects that might block its signal, such as walls or furniture. The router translates the information from the computer and sends it through a cable to a modem.

Wi-Fi Friendly U.S. Cities

These cities have the most hotspots for Wi-Fi users.
1. New York, New York
2. Austin, Texas
3. Los Angeles, California
4. Atlanta, Georgia
5. Chicago, Illinois

Source: WeFi.com

Going Wireless

The only thing that is possibly better than a wireless computer is a wireless video game. The GameCube for Nintendo in 2003 was the first popular console that had a wireless remote control. Three years later, Nintendo introduced the Wii. As players move the wireless controller, the figure on the screen moves as well. PlayStation Move for PS3 also has a wireless wand, or controller. Its movements are tracked by a camera on the console.

In 2010, Xbox 360 introduced Kinect. This is not only wireless—it drops the controller altogether. Kinect uses an infrared camera that instantly tracks the movements of the player's body and hands. When a player moves, the figure on the screen moves the same way. Who knows what the next wireless innovation will be?

The **modem** links a computer to the Internet. It changes the digital information in the computer to a form that can be sent through phone or cable television lines. The signal goes to servers that change the signals back into a digital form. These servers are joined to form a network—the Internet. To receive Internet through Wi-Fi, the process works in reverse. A signal goes from the Internet to a modem to a router to a computer.

For Wi-Fi to work properly, the computer should be no more than about 120 feet from the router. Outdoors, the maximum distance is around 300 to 500 feet. That allows people to use Wi-Fi outdoors in public spaces like a park, as well as in **cafes** and **restaurants** with hotspots.

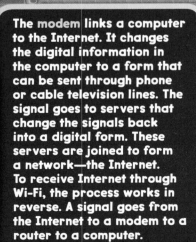

HOW to Make Your Own Camera

The oldest and cheapest camera ever made is the camera obscura. Camera obscura means "dark chamber," which describes this simple device. A camera obscura is a dark room with a small hole in one wall. Light reflects off an object outside the wall. The light passes through the hole and makes an upside-down image of the object on the opposite wall. The image is very clear because a tiny hole focuses light. If the hole were large, the light hitting the wall would scatter and make the image of the object look blurry.

A camera obscura can only show what is directly outside the room. To view something else, you'd have to carry the room around. Since that isn't very practical, people made small, portable versions of the device, like the one in the photo above. And so can you.

What You Need

- An empty can shaped like a cylinder, with a metal bottom, such as a potato-chip can
- Wax paper or white tissue paper
- Thumbtack or push pin
- Masking or electrical tape
- Ruler
- Marker
- Utility knife (ask an adult to use it)
- Aluminum foil

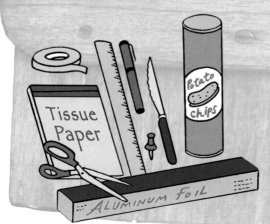

What to Do

1 With the ruler, measure two inches up from the bottom of the can in two places and mark the spots. Connect the marks so the line goes around the can. Have an adult cut the can into two pieces along the line.

2 Use a thumbtack or pushpin to make a tiny hole in the center of the metal bottom of the can. Spin the tack in the hole to smooth the sides of the hole.

3 Cut out a circle of wax paper or tissue paper. Place it as tightly as possible over the open top of the short part of the can and tape it into place.

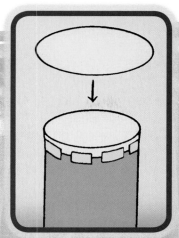

4 Place the long part of the can over the short part. Tape the two parts of the can together so it looks like it did before you cut it.

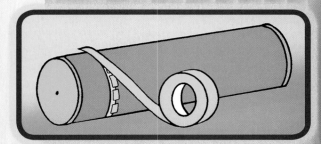

5 Wrap aluminum foil around the can, lining up the edges with the top and bottom of the can. If there is extra foil at the top, fold it into the can. Make sure no light enters the can except through the hole in the bottom and the opening at the top.

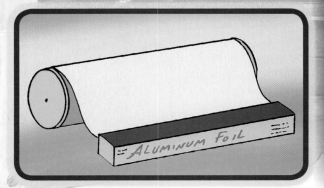

6 Place an object under bright light, point the pinhole at it, and view through the opening. Place your hands around the opening to keep out light. You should see the object on the wax paper, but upside down. Move your camera closer or farther away until the object is in focus.

Taking pictures with a digital camera is a snap. Still, to take good photos, it pays to explore what your camera can do.

- Most digital cameras have a flash. Sometimes the flash creates glare and can make a harsh light. Learn when to turn off the flash and use natural light.

- A camera with a rotating lens lets you take pictures at different angles. You can even take a picture of yourself.

- If your camera comes with a burst mode, you can take several pictures in a row without waiting for the camera to recharge. This is good for shooting sports events.

- When you shoot, try not to put the subject at the center of the photo.

- Use the horizontal lines in the view screen to make sure the picture is level.

- Don't be afraid to take a bad photo. After all, you can always delete it and try again.

HOW to Make a Periscope

On a submarine, a periscope lets the captain see what's happening above the waves while the sub stays hidden underwater. Soldiers in tanks peer through periscopes to see outside. If you're stuck behind a crowd, a periscope lets you look over people's heads. With a periscope, you can see over walls and around corners without being seen. It's the perfect tool for a spy or to watch a parade if you're not in the front row.

A periscope is a tube with a mirror at both ends. The mirrors are angled so light bounces off the upper mirror, goes down the tube, and reflects off the bottom mirror into the eyes of the viewer. The longer the tube, the smaller the image a viewer sees. In submarines, periscope tubes are very long, so they are fitted with magnifying lenses instead of mirrors. Smaller periscopes are easy to build. Scope it out.

What You Need

- 2 clean, one-quart milk or juice cartons
- 2 small mirrors (The mirrors don't have to be the same size. If either is too small to fit in the carton, tape the mirror to a piece of cardboard.)
- Scissors
- Tape
- Ruler
- An adult to help you

What to Do

1 Cut off the tops off both cartons.

2 Cut out an opening near the bottom of each box. There should be about one-quarter of an inch of carton on three sides of the opening.

3 Place one carton on its side on a table, with the opening facing right. Measure up 2¾ inches from the left edge of the carton. Mark that spot with a pencil. Draw a diagonal line from the bottom right corner of the carton to the mark on the left edge.

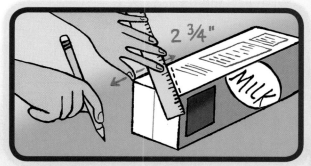

4 Use the point of the scissors (or have a parent use a straight-edge tool) to cut along the diagonal line you drew. Don't cut all the way to the left or right edges of the carton. Cut just enough so the mirror will fit into the slot.

5 Slide the mirror in the slot you cut so the reflecting side faces out the opening. Tape it loosely into place against the bottom of the opening. Hold the carton upright, with the top pointed at the ceiling. Look in the mirror. You should see the ceiling. If not, adjust the mirror, then tape it more firmly.

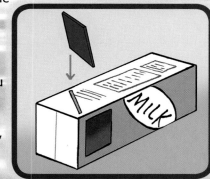

6 Repeat steps 3, 4, and 5 with the other carton.

7 Place the two cartons on the table. One opening should be at the bottom, facing you. The other opening should be at the top, facing away from you. Squeeze the open end of one carton and slide it into the other carton. Tape them together.

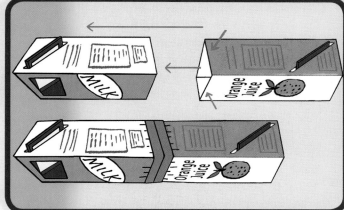

8 You can do plenty of things with your periscope. Hold it up to see over a fence. Hold it sideways to see around corners. Open a door and use the periscope to see what's in a room without going in. Look through the top mirror to see under tables or beds.

HOW Does Popcorn Pop?

No one knows for sure who invented popcorn. But we do know that it was first made in the New World—because that was the place corn first grew. (Who first put salt and butter on popcorn is also a mystery that may never be solved!)

Scientists have found grains of popcorn preserved in places in South America and in Mexico. Some of the popcorn was thousands of years old.

Another mystery about popcorn is what makes it pop. A Native American legend has an explanation: popcorn pops because of a demon hidden inside the kernel. Every time the corn is heated over a fire, the demon gets angry. As the corn gets hotter and hotter, the demon gets madder and madder. Finally, the demon blows his top, making the popcorn explode. Then the tiny demon can escape.

Of course, there isn't a kernel of truth to this legend. The real reason has to do with science, not the supernatural.

Popcorn kernels are actually corn seeds. The seed is surrounded by a thin, hard, protective shell, or hull. Inside each kernel is a tiny embryo, the part of a seed that develops into a plant, as well as starch. This blob of starch feeds the embryo.

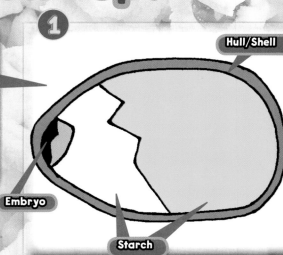

1

Hull/Shell

Embryo

Starch

As the temperature rises, the water in the starch beg to boil and expand, or spread out. The starch turns to liquid. As the temperature nears 400°F, the water turns to steam, which pushes against the hard shell. pressure of the steam finally makes the shell split o and explode.

3

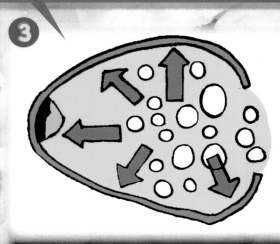

Food fuels your body and gives you the nutrients you need. Best of all, food tastes good! Here's the skinny on some chow that we love to eat.

Steamed Up

It's the pressure of steam that makes popcorn pop. If you don't believe that, try these three experiments before you make popcorn.

1 Gently crack some popcorn kernels by pressing against them with the bottom of a pan. When you try to heat the kernels, they won't pop. The cracks in the shell prevent pressure from building up inside.

2 Heat the kernels first in low temperature (below 300°F). The kernels won't pop because there isn't enough heat to make steam.

3 Place the kernels in a warm oven or in the sun for a few days before trying to pop them. The kernels need to be about 14 percent moisture. The heat will dry out the moisture and the kernels won't pop.

Starch contains water. When the popcorn is heated, the water in the starch begins to get hot too. The heat turns the starch into a jelly-like material

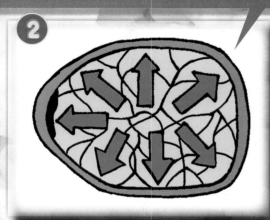

The steamy explosion turns the liquid starch into tiny foam-like bubbles. The bubbles connect into bigger bubbles, which take up 40 times the space of the original starch blob. The water in the starch completely boils off, so the starch bubbles quickly dry in the warm air. And you have popcorn.

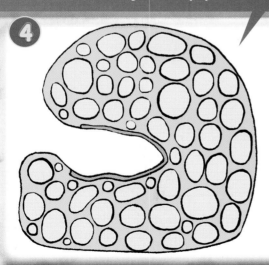

FACTOID

Most of the corn used to make popcorn is grown in Nebraska and Indiana.

HOW Does Bread Rise?

"Dough" and "bread" are slang for money. That's not so strange. Bread has been valuable in many cultures over the centuries. It has even been called "the staff of life," meaning it is an important part of our diet.

There are two kinds of bread: flat bread and leavened (*leh*-vend) bread, which is bread that rises. Either type of bread can be used to make everyone's favorite food invention: the sandwich. In 1729, an Englishman, the Earl of Sandwich, had the idea to place food between two slices of bread. Hundreds of years later, his creation really took off when sliced bread was invented.

Today, Americans eat about 45 billion sandwiches every year, and spend more than $100 billion on them. That's a lot of dough!

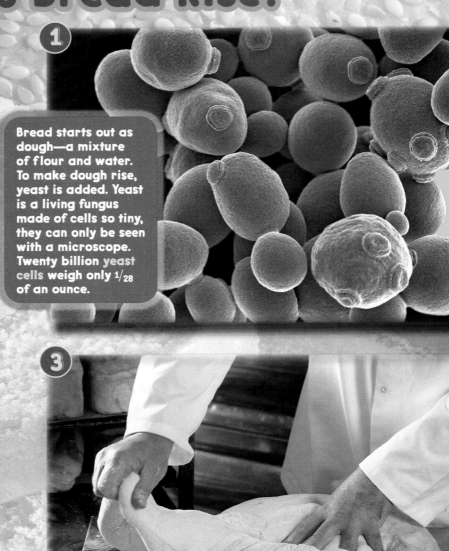

1 Bread starts out as dough—a mixture of flour and water. To make dough rise, yeast is added. Yeast is a living fungus made of cells so tiny, they can only be seen with a microscope. Twenty billion yeast cells weigh only $1/28$ of an ounce.

3 To make it rise even more, the dough is kneaded (*need*-ed) or mixed. Within the flour is a network of stringy proteins called gluten (*glue*-tin). When the dough is kneaded, the strands of gluten become stronger. The carbon dioxide gas makes the gluten stretch. Since the gas can't escape, it forces the dough to expand.

2

Dry yeast is dormant, or inactive, until it is put in water and sugar. Sugar is yeast's favorite food, and when yeast cells gobble the sweet stuff, they give off carbon dioxide gas. The carbon dioxide makes the dough puff up.

4

Dough is often allowed to "rest" after it's kneaded. As the dough relaxes, it may expand many times its original size. When the dough is placed in a hot oven, the heat makes the yeast go wild. It produces even more carbon dioxide, raising the bread more. Soon the heat kills the yeast cells, and the bread stops rising. So when you bite into bread, you aren't eating living fungus—you are swallowing dead yeast cells!

Loafing Around

Certain breads are often associated with particular countries. Can you match the bread to the nation it comes from? The answers are upside down below.

1. Soda bread
2. Black bread
3. Baguette
4. Tortilla
5. Crisp bread
6. Pita bread
7. Bread sticks
8. Matzah
9. Naan
10. Cornbread

A. Russia
B. Italy
C. Israel
D. United States
E. India
F. Sweden
G. Mexico
H. Lebanon
I. France
J. Ireland

1.J,2.A,3.I,4.G,5.F,6.H,7.B,8.C,9.E,10.D

Gas Up!

Yeast isn't the only ingredient that makes baked goods rise. Baking soda and baking powder are chemicals that combine with water to give off carbon dioxide gas. Baking soda also needs an acid, such as yogurt or chocolate, to work. Baking soda is used to raise cakes, cookies, pancakes, and some breads. Baking powder is used in muffins, cakes, and biscuits.

FACTOID

Talk about a hero sandwich. The record for the longest loaf of bread is 3,600 feet. Eighteen bakers in Modica, Italy, used 2,500 pounds of flour to bake it.

HOW Is Chocolate Made?

Just about everyone loves chocolate. The average American eats about 12 pounds of it each year. Britons and the Swiss eat almost twice as much chocolate. This popular treat starts out as seeds found on a cacao (ka-*cow*) tree. Cacao trees grow in tropical countries near the equator, such as the Ivory Coast and Ghana in Africa, Brazil in South America, and Indonesia in Asia. Pods on the cacao tree grow to be the size of melons. Inside the pods are seeds, or beans. Chocolate is made from these beans.

Cacao beans from different trees have different tastes. Sometimes chocolate makers produce a chocolate product using a single type of bean. Some chocolate makers combine beans from different countries to get the taste they want. Turning these beans into mouth-watering chocolate is a long process—but it's worth the time and effort!

1

2

The whitish pulp on the beans helps them ferment, or go through chemical changes, which gives them a better taste. After fermenting, the beans are dried in the sun or put in special ovens. The dried beans are put in bags and shipped to factories across the globe.

In a year, a cacao tree can produce 30 to 40 pods. Inside each pod is between 20 to 40 seeds, or cacao beans. Workers cut or knock the pods off the trees by hand, scoop out the pulp-covered beans, and put them in baskets.

3

At a chocolate factory, the beans are heated in roasters. Roasted beans, like the ones in the person's hand, have loose shells and a richer flavor. Next, a hulling machine separates the shell from the bean's chocolatey heart, called the nib.

4

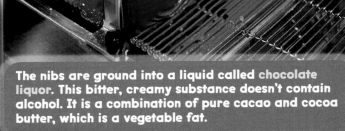

The nibs are ground into a liquid called chocolate liquor. This bitter, creamy substance doesn't contain alcohol. It is a combination of pure cacao and cocoa butter, which is a vegetable fat.

5

To make milk chocolate, milk and sugar are added to the chocolate liquor. The mixture is dried, becoming a brown powder called chocolate crumb. The crumb moves through steel rollers that grind the mixture into a thick paste.

6

The paste is poured into a machine, called a conch (kongk), that grinds the paste into a smooth liquid. Nuts or other ingredients are sometimes added to the chocolate. Then it is poured into molds to shape them into bars, chips, or other forms and shipped out to chocolate lovers everywhere.

HOW Is Ice Cream Made?

"I scream, you scream, we all scream for ice cream." Actually, only 98 percent of all American households scream for ice cream. Every year, each American on average eats about 16 quarts of ice cream. Americans spend about $12 billion on the cool stuff annually.

Many experts believe Emperor Nero of ancient Rome ordered the first frozen dessert. Others say icy desserts were served much earlier in Asian countries. Today, most ice cream is made in large factories, using buttermilk, milk solids (that's everything in milk except the fat and water), sugar, and chemicals that prevent ice crystals from forming when ice cream is frozen. What's the favorite flavor of ice cream? Vanilla, a three-to-one choice over runner-up chocolate.

1 At a typical ice cream factory, huge amounts of ingredients arrive every day. Liquid ingredients, such as milk, cream, and vanilla (see inset), are pumped into a large tank. Dry ingredients, such as cocoa for chocolate ice cream, are placed into big hoppers. The dry and liquid ingredients are then blended to create an ice cream mix.

2 The ice cream mix travels to the pasteurizing section. The temperature of the mix is raised to 150°F for about 30 minutes, which kills any germs.

③

In a blending machine, the mix is cooled down and stirred until it's smooth. Ingredients such as nuts and chocolate chips are added and mixed evenly. That way they won't sink to the bottom. In this photo, a container of chocolate fudge is being emptied. It will be added to the vanilla ice cream mixture to make a fudgey product.

④

The ice cream mix, now as thick as a milk shake, is pumped into freezing chambers. When the temperature of the mix reaches 21°F, it becomes ice cream. Machines pour the ice cream into containers and place a lid on them. Conveyor belts move the ice cream to a hardening room. Here, the ice cream is frozen to a temperature of -20°F.

⑤

The ice cream containers are sent to a cold warehouse, where they are wrapped and loaded onto trucks with freezers. The containers are shipped to stores across the country.

TOP 5 Ice Cream Consuming Countries in the World

1. United States
2. New Zealand
3. Denmark
4. Australia
5. Belgium/Luxembourg

Source: foodchannel.com

HOW Do Chili Peppers Make Your Mouth Burn?

Bite into a chili pepper and within seconds your lips feel like they're burning. How does a chili set off a three-alarm fire in your mouth?

The answer is a chemical inside the pepper called capsaicin (cap-*say*-sin). No other plant contains this oil. It has no odor or color. Capsaicin sets off heat and pain sensors on sensitive areas of your skin, including the tongue, throat, and lips. The sensors tell your brain that your mouth is on fire, even though there is no rise in temperature. Your face gets red and you begin to sweat. Your fire sensors have sent out a false alarm!

Not all peppers are alike. Some are super hot. Other peppers have no burn at all. So before you swallow a chili pepper, find out what kind it is.

FACTOID

Birds spread the seeds of wild chilies. The birds don't have pain receptors in their mouths so the capsaicin doesn't bother them.

Inside the Chili Pepper

The calyx (ka-*licks*) protects the flower before it opens.

Chilies grow from seeds, but the seeds don't produce capsaicin. They are hot only because some capsaicin from the nearby capsaicin glands rubs off on them.

The capsaicin glands are found between the placenta and the inner wall. These tiny sacs produce the capsaicin that causes the burn. The hottest part is near the top of the pepper, close to the seeds. To get rid of most of the heat in a pepper, remove the ribs.

The placenta is a vein that runs the length of the chili. The seeds are attached to this, especially at the upper part.

The endocarp is the inside layer of the pepper. It surrounds the seeds.

The mesocarp is the middle layer of the pepper. It is thick and contains the most water.

The skin, or outside layer, of the pepper is called the exocarp.

The apex contains the least amount of capsaicin.

The pedicle is the stem of the pepper.

Putting Out the Fire

Capsaicin is so strong, you could put a drop of the stuff into 100,000 drops of water, drink it, and still taste the heat. Water won't put out this fire. It just spreads the oil—and the hot sensation.

Instead, drink milk or tomato juice, or eat bread, rice, yogurt, ice cream, or salt. They absorb the oil. Wear rubber gloves if you handle a pepper. If you touch a pepper, especially the ribs, wash your hands with soap and water. Otherwise, you might spread that burning sensation to other parts of your body.

The Heat Is On

The heat of a pepper is measured in Scoville units. It was named after the creator of the scale, Wilbur Scoville. The higher the number of units, the hotter the pepper. Peppers of the same type vary, so they may contain different amounts of capsaicin. That's why each pepper has a range of Scoville units.

Pure capsaicin: 15,000,000–16,000,000

Type of Pepper	Scoville Units
Naga viper	1,359,000
Bhut Jolokia (also called Naga Jolokia or Ghost Chile)	850,000–1,000,000
Habanero chile	100,000–350,000
Scotch bonnet	100,000–325,000
Jamaican hot pepper	100,000–200,000
Thai pepper	50,000–100,000
Cayenne pepper	30,000–50,000
Serrano pepper	5,000–23,000
Jalapeño pepper	2,500–8,000
Poblano pepper	1,000–2,000
Bell pepper	0

HOW to Make Pizza

Pizza is one of the most popular foods in the U.S. And it's the favorite food of American kids ages 3 to 11. What we call pizza started out centuries ago as flat bread topped with herbs. Then, in the 1700s, in Naples, Italy, someone got the bright idea of putting tomatoes on the bread. Cheese was the next brainstorm, and the rest is pizza history. Today pizza is topped with endless ingredients, from shrimp and peanut butter to refried beans and pineapples.

Like most breads, pizza is made with yeast to give the dough a light, crunchy feel. Before you make pizza dough, check to see if the yeast is active, or alive. When warm water is added to yeast, the mixture should produce bubbles after a few minutes. That means the yeast is okay. If there are no bubbles, the yeast is inactive and should not be used.

FACTOIDS

○ About 3 billion pizzas are sold in the United States every year.

○ The first pizzeria to open in the United States was Lombardi's in New York City, in 1905. It still serves pizza.

What You Need

- 1 package active dry yeast
- 1 cup warm water
- 1 tablespoon sugar
- 1 teaspoon salt
- 3 cups flour
- Olive oil or vegetable oil
- Extra flour for kneading the dough
- Two large cookie sheets or baking pans
- Pizza toppings such as tomato sauce, cheese, sausage, vegetables

What to Do

1 Put the yeast into a large bowl, add the water and sugar, and let stand for about 5 minutes. The mixture should start bubbling. Stir in the salt.

2 Add all the flour to the bowl and mix it until the dough forms a ball. You might need to lightly dust the dough and your hands with flour if the dough is too sticky.

3 Lightly dust a cutting board or smooth surface with flour and put the dough ball on it. Knead the ball with your hands, pushing and pulling, for no more than five minutes, until the ball is smooth and elastic. If necessary, add small amounts of flour to make the kneading easier.

4 Put the dough in a bowl and cover it with plastic wrap or a towel. Let the dough sit on a counter at room temperature until it doubles in size.

5 Take out the dough and punch it down with your fist. Shape it into a ball, and use a butter knife to cut the ball into two even portions. They should be fairly round. Lightly oil both pans and place the dough on each. Use your hands or a rolling pin to stretch out each ball. Make the dough as thick or thin as you like.

 Pizza Toppings

Americans gobble 350 slices of pizza every second! Pizza makers have tried almost every type of topping: peanut butter and jelly, bacon, even mashed potatoes. Still, nothing beats good old pepperoni. Here are the tasty favorites according to a study.

1. **Pepperoni**
2. **Mushrooms**
3. **Sausage**
4. **Green pepper**
5. **Onion**

Source: Publications International, LTD.

6 Have an adult pre-heat the oven to 420°F. In the meantime, put whatever toppings you want on the pizza, such as tomato sauce, cheese, sausage slices, meatballs, mushrooms, onions…. Let a parent slide the pizza pans into the oven and cook the pies until the crusts are golden brown, about 15 to 20 minutes.

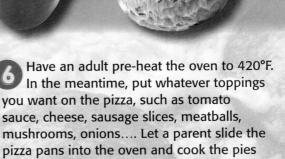

HOW to Make Ice Cream

People have been enjoying ice cream for thousands of years, although it may not have looked like our version. Early ice cream was probably more like flavored ices or soft cream cooled on a bed of ice.

The American colonists gave the cool treat the name ice cream (cream that was iced). In those days, ice cream was made by turning cream by hand in a wooden container. The container was kept cold by a mixture of salt and ice, which lowered the temperature below freezing. Today, ice cream lovers can make their own with an electric-powered ice cream maker. But you don't need a fancy machine to make ice cream.

TOP 5 Favorite Ice Cream Flavors

FLAVOR	PERCENT OF PEOPLE WHO PREFER IT
1. Vanilla	29 %
2. Chocolate	8.9 %
3. Butter pecan	5.3 %
4. Strawberry	5.3 %
5. Neapolitan	4.2 %

Source: International Ice Cream Association

What You Need

- 2 tablespoons sugar
- ½ teaspoon vanilla extract
- 1 cup of milk or half & half
- ¾ cup rock salt
- 1 quart-size ziplock freezer bag
- 1 gallon-size ziplock freezer bag
- Crushed ice
- Kitchen shears or regular scissors

What to Do

1 Combine the first three ingredients in a medium-size bowl. Stir until the sugar completely dissolves and you can't see any grains. Put the mix into the 1-quart ziplock bag and seal it carefully.

2 Place about half of the rock salt and about 2 cups of crushed ice into the 1-gallon ziplock bag. Put the 1-quart bag into the larger bag and zip it tight.

3 Place the bag on a flat surface and flip it gently end over end. Do this for five minutes. Open the 1-gallon bag over a sink and drain the water. Don't let any rock salt or ice fall out.

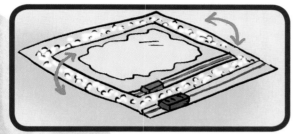

4 Refill the bag with the rest of the rock salt and the crushed ice. Gently flip the bag again, end over end, for 15 minutes. If your arms get tired, take a one-minute break. Or have someone else help out with the flipping.

5 Open the 1-gallon bag over the sink and drain the water. Remove the 1-quart bag and throw away the larger bag. Dry off the outside of the 1-quart bag and snip off a corner with scissors. Squeeze the ice cream into a bowl and dig in! After you've made vanilla ice cream, experiment with other flavors by adding crushed nuts or fruit juices, such as grape juice.

Yo! It's Yogurt!

Yogurt is another popular dairy-based treat. To make yogurt, bacteria is added to milk and then heated. The living bacteria in yogurt can help keep your digestive system healthy. Here's how to make yogurt.

What You Need
- 1 quart warm milk
- ½ cup plain yogurt with live cultures
- Glass bowl
- Whisk or spoon
- Glass casserole dish with lid or glass baking dish with lid

What to Do
1. Heat an oven to 100°F.

2. Mix or whisk 1-quart warm milk and ½ cup yogurt in a bowl.

3. Place the mixture into the baking dish, cover it, and have a parent put it into the oven.

4. Turn off the oven and let the mixture sit overnight. You've got yogurt. Add honey, jam, or pieces of fruit for sweetness, and nuts or trail mix for crunch.

HOW Can We Protect Earth from Big Space Rocks?

Every day, 100 tons of asteroids and comets land on the surface of Earth. Almost all of these pieces are too tiny to cause harm. But much larger rocks have struck Earth. Millions of years ago, a rock about a mile and a half wide and weighing 10 billion tons hit what is now Manson, Illinois. It created a crater three miles deep and about 18 miles wide. Glaciers smoothed over the crater, so it's no longer visible. About 65 million years ago, a huge comet hit near Mexico, leaving a crater 110 miles across. Its blast may have wiped out the dinosaurs.

Can we get hit again by a large meteor or asteroid? According to scientists, about 320,000 asteroids larger than 300 feet across orbit within our solar system. If any one of them hit Earth, it would be a disaster. Scientists think that none of those rocks will collide with our planet during the next few hundred thousand years. But if one of them did head towards Earth, how could we avoid getting hit? Scientists are coming up with plans to keep Earth safe.

Early Warning: To keep Earth safe from comets and asteroids, scientists first have to pinpoint where the rocks are. NASA's Near Earth Object Program is locating and tracking at least 90 percent of space rocks larger than 450 feet in our solar system.

Bad Breakup: Scientists wouldn't blast a space rock to pieces with a nuclear missile. Those pieces could hit Earth and cause just as much damage. But a nuclear blast set off near a small rock might completely vaporize it.

People have always kept their eyes on the skies. But thanks to powerful telescopes, space probes, and brave astronauts, our knowledge of heavenly bodies is at an all-time high.

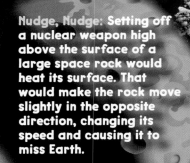

Nudge, Nudge: Setting off a nuclear weapon high above the surface of a large space rock would heat its surface. That would make the rock move slightly in the opposite direction, changing its speed and causing it to miss Earth.

Hot Spot: Instead of using a nuclear blast to nudge the space object, laser beams from a spacecraft would do the trick.

Catching Rays: One bright idea is to place large solar sails on the space object. Rays from the sun would push against the surface of the sails and slowly redirect the object away from Earth.

Mutual Attraction: A large unmanned spacecraft could be put in orbit around a space rock. The gravity of both objects would attract each other. This would change the path of the space rock enough to avoid Earth.

Rocking Russia

On June 30, 1908, a huge explosion took place in Tunguska, a remote part of Russia. The blast knocked down trees for 20 miles. People living 250 miles from the explosion saw a huge fireball that rose 12 miles in the sky. An area of several hundred square miles was scorched. The sound of the blast was heard 500 miles away.

Scientists think the explosion was caused by a comet or an asteroid about 500 feet wide and weighing 7 million tons. As the object sped through Earth's atmosphere, it heated up and exploded about five miles above the ground. No fragments were left behind. Fortunately, the object burst over an unpopulated area (as seen today, below).

HOW Will the Juno Probe Uncover Jupiter's Secrets?

Jupiter is the largest planet in the solar system, and it holds some big secrets. Scientists don't know for sure what's going on under the gas giant's 621-mile-thick atmosphere. That may change in 2016, when the unmanned *Juno* spacecraft is scheduled to reach Jupiter after traveling five years. *Juno* will come within 3,000 miles of Jupiter's cloud tops—which, in space terms, is very close. Over one year, *Juno* will send back information during 32 orbits of the planet, including the first clear pictures of the planet's poles.

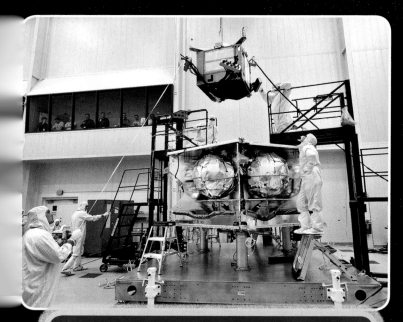

NASA scientists put together the *Juno* spacecraft. They hope it will help reveal the history of Jupiter and the solar system.

The spacecraft will get its power from solar panels. They will stretch out more than 66 feet to gather sunlight that's 25 times weaker than light striking Earth.

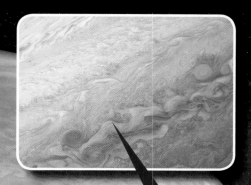

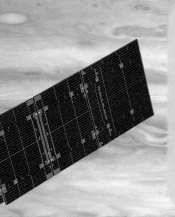

Fact File: Jupiter

Jupiter is the largest planet of the solar system. Covered by swirling clouds, the planet is made mostly of hydrogen and helium in the form of gas and liquid. Here are more facts about the fifth planet from the sun.

Diameter: 88,650 miles (11 times greater than Earth's diameter)

Average distance from the sun: 483,682,810 miles

Average distance from Earth: 391,463,851 miles

Average surface temperature: -238°F

Surface gravity: 214 times that of Earth's

Length of day: 9.93 hours

Length of year: 11.87 Earth years

Number of moons: 62

Number of rings: 3

Instruments aboard the craft will record data that might explain what Jupiter's clouds are made of, how thick they are, how they move, and why winds blow them at speeds up to 372 miles per hour.

Jupiter

Juno will map Jupiter's powerful magnetic field, which spreads far out into space, as shown here. This information may offer clues about what the planet's core is made of.

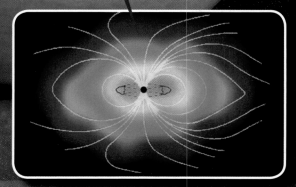

The Missing Belt

The atmosphere of Jupiter is made up of light-colored layers of clouds called bands and dark layers called belts. These layers last for many years. But recently, a giant belt had suddenly disappeared, and no one knew why. Then, months later, the belt began to reappear. Experts think that the belt had just been covered by white clouds driven by powerful winds. Now it seems the higher white clouds are drifting away to reveal the darker belt beneath.

HOW Do Astronauts Train?

Since the early days of space exploration, astronauts have landed on the moon, walked in space, performed experiments on the space shuttle, and spent time on the International Space Station.

Here's a look at some of the training astronauts get at the Lyndon B. Johnson Space Center, in Houston, Texas. Some of these astronauts may one day return to the moon—or blast off for Mars.

Astronauts-in-training learn aircraft safety, including how to eject and parachute from a plane. They also take flight training. Space pilots have learned to fly aircraft built to work like the space shuttle.

FACTOID

How do you become an astronaut? Here are some requirements:

○ An astronaut must be a college graduate, with a major in technology, math, or other science fields.

○ Many astronauts are pilots in the military, but civilians who have never flown can be astronauts too. These astronauts are called mission specialists, and they can be engineers, scientists, doctors, or researchers.

○ An astronaut must be between 5 feet, four inches and six feet, four inches tall, and be a U.S. citizen.

Astronauts train for hours in a huge tank of water, which gives the feel of weightlessness. They do tasks in the water that they will do in zero gravity during space flight. One tank, the Neutral Buoyancy Laboratory, is 200 feet long and 40 feet deep. It's the largest indoor pool in the world.

To experience weightlessness, astronauts ride on airplanes that go high up and then dive. For 30 seconds during each dive, astronauts float around the cabin in zero-gravity conditions.

Candidates receive survival training. They are taught how to stay alive if their craft lands in the ocean or in a forest. They experience tough challenges so they know what to do in a real situation.

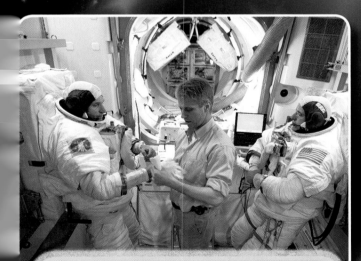

A crew of astronauts practices living and working in mockups—exact copies of the spacecraft they'll fly. They also train in simulators that reproduce the events of a mission. Trainers give the crew problems to solve or put them in emergency situations to overcome.

The people on the ground who give information and instructions to astronauts during missions are called the flight-control team. An astronaut crew practices an upcoming mission with a particular flight-control team. That way, the actual flight will run smoothly.

HOW Does the Sun Stay Hot?

The temperature of the sun's surface is about 10,000°F. At its core, the sun is more than 27,000,000°F. The ancient Greeks believed the sun's heat came from a huge lump of coal that burned in its center. In the 1800s, some scientists thought the sun was filled with erupting volcanoes. Others believed the sun got hot from millions of meteorites striking it.

The sun started out as a massive ball of gas and dust. About 4.5 billion years ago, gravity squeezed together the particles so tightly, they produced heat—and the sun was born. But how does it continue to burn? Inside the sun, the intense heat at its birth started a process called nuclear fusion. Nuclear fusion happens when hydrogen atoms in the sun's core combine, or fuse, to form the element helium. This releases energy, which reaches Earth (93 million miles away) mostly in the form of light and heat. The sun has plenty of hydrogen, so it should keep us warm for about 5 billion more years.

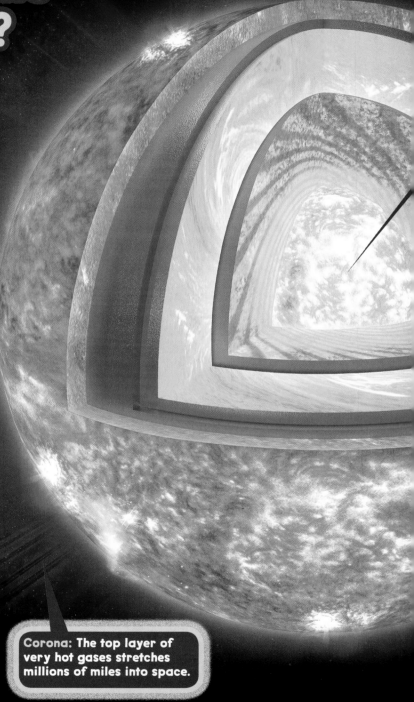

Corona: The top layer of very hot gases stretches millions of miles into space.

Core: The center takes up only two percent of the sun's space, but holds 60 percent of its mass. Here, immense heat and pressure slam together parts of hydrogen atoms. The atoms fuse into helium atoms, releasing almost all the energy that keeps the sun shining.

Radiative Zone: The energy from the core rises in the form of particles called photons (*foh*-tahnz). Here, the energy of the photons is absorbed by various atoms. Those atoms then give off more energy. This way, energy slowly rises to the convective zone.

Convective Zone: In this layer, energy heats currents of gas, which rise to the surface of the sun. As the energy is released at the surface, the gas cools and falls back down.

Photosphere: This 200-mile-thick layer of swirling gas is the surface of the sun. The light that we see comes from this layer.

Chromosphere: From here, huge jets and sheets of hot gases rise above the surface of the sun and fall back.

Sun Safety

Sunlight is the reason there's life on Earth. But sunlight's ultraviolet (UV) rays can also give you a sunburn. Follow these tips to keep your skin safe during the day.

- Stay in the shade, especially between 10 a.m. and 4 p.m., when the sun's rays are strongest.

- Whenever you're out in the sun, even for a short walk, wear sunscreen with at least a 30 SPF rating. Use it year-round, not just in the summer.

- When you're outside, cover up. Wear clothes that sunlight can't go through. Place a hand inside the clothes: If you can see your hand, the cloth isn't thick enough.

- Protect your eyes. Wear sunglasses with labels that say the glasses have 100 percent UV protection. Wear a wide-brim hat that shades your eyes, ears, and face.

- Don't forget your lips: Apply a lip balm that has an SPF of at least 15.

HOW Do We Know if There's Another Earth Out There?

It took observers thousands of years to discover all the planets in our solar system. But no one knew if any planets circled other stars—until 1995. That's when the first exoplanets were found. An exoplanet is a planet that orbits a star other than our own star, the sun. Since then, nearly 500 more exoplanets have been found.

Could there be life on one of these exoplanets? The answer so far is maybe. Astronomers may have found one Earth-size planet in a star's "Goldilocks region." In this zone, things are not too hot, not too cold, but just right for life. Scientists are questioning whether this planet could harbor life. In the meantime, they keep looking. There are so many stars out there, there must be warm, watery Earth-like worlds orbiting some of them. And perhaps there is Earth-like life on one of those worlds.

Goldilocks Worlds: Where Things Are Just Right for Life

SOLAR SYSTEM

Habitable (Goldilocks) zone

The hot zone

Too Close: If a planet gets too close to a star, the heat can make all its water boil off, as happened to Mercury. The star can also warm a planet's surface to deadly temperatures, which was the fate of Venus.

FACTOID
Earth is just the right distance from the sun to support life. If it were 5 percent closer, all the water on Earth would have boiled away. If it were 15 percent farther away, all the water would be frozen.

Exo-llent Search!

For most of human history, we've known only about the planets that circle our sun. In the past 20 years, scientists have found 492 other planets orbiting distant stars. Most are giants compared with Earth. But new ways of searching are making it easier to find smaller ones—the kind where life may exist.

Exoplanets Discovered

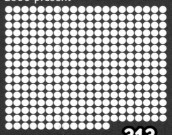

Pre-2000
31

2000-05
148

2006-present
313

Total: **492** *
Possible Earth-like worlds found so far: **1**

* As of January 1, 2011

Source: The Extrasolar Planets Encyclopedia, with data from California & Carnegie Planet Search, Geneva Extrasolar Search Program, University of Texas, and others

The Artist's Eye: This Earth-like world does not exist, but similar ones are probably out there.

STAR

The cold zone

Too Far: Space is a cold place. A planet doesn't have to be too far from its sun to become frigid and have its water freeze solid. Atmosphere holds in heat, and Mars might be a living world today if it had kept its atmosphere.

Just Right: Earth exists in the livable (Goldilocks) zone, where plenty of liquid water can be present. There may be different forms of life on other planets that orbit in a Goldilocks zone.

HOW to Build a Planetarium

The best way to see the Milky Way is to gaze up at the sky on a cloudless night. The next best way is to go to a planetarium. A planetarium is a theater where heavenly bodies are projected onto a dome-shaped screen. The device that projects the stars and planets is also called a planetarium. The first modern planetarium was built in 1924. It was a projector that shined lights through hundreds of tiny holes onto a wall to stand for stars.

Planetariums now use computers and high-tech projectors to show the positions of the stars and planets on any given night—past, present, and future. Many planetariums also have digital projection systems that can take viewers on a tour of the planets, show the birth of the solar system, and much more. Put on your own star show by making an out-of-this-world planetarium.

What You Need
- Empty cereal box
- Several 3-inch-by-5-inch index cards
- Pencil
- Flashlight
- Tape
- Scissors

What to Do

1 Cut out a rectangle in the underside of the cereal box. Make it a bit smaller than the index cards. The top of the box should be open.

2 Use the pencil to punch holes in the index cards in the shape of constellations. Two constellations are drawn to help get you started (see "Constellations"). You can find other constellations online or in a reference book.

FACTOID

The earliest type of planetarium was a mechanical device called an orrery (or-er-ree). It rotated and revolved small globes that represented the sun and planets.

3 Tape one of the index cards over the bottom of the cereal box.

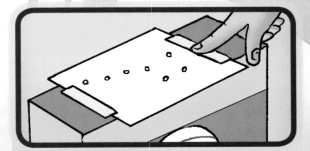

4 Turn off the lights—the room should be dark. Stand a few feet from a blank wall. Hold the cereal box so the end with the index card is pointed toward the wall. Through the open end, shine the flashlight inside the cereal box at a 45 degree angle.

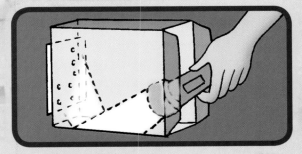

5 View the stars shining brightly on your wall. Use other index cards with constellations to create new star shows.

Constellations

In ancient times, people looked at the night sky and noticed groups of stars. When they connected these stars with lines, the groups looked like people, animals, or objects. These clusters of stars are called constellations. Below are two of the 88 recognized constellations. Use these pictures to create index cards for your planetarium. Don't forget to label each constellation you make.

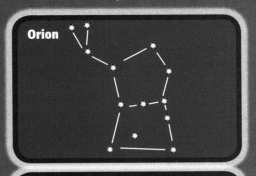

Orion

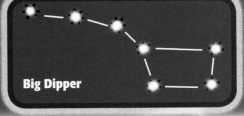

Big Dipper

FACTOID

The Hayden Sphere, in New York City, uses a one-of-a-kind high-definition projector and a powerful virtual reality simulator to create amazing, realistic shows. You can see programs that take you on a journey to a star, show cosmic collisions, and search for life in the universe.

HOW to Launch a Rocket

The first rockets ever launched were fireworks, set off in China more than a thousand years ago. The fireworks used the power of gun powder to take off. It wasn't until the mid-1900s that people began to build rockets to travel into space.

A space rocket needs a lot of power to lift off and escape Earth's gravity. The power comes from huge engines that burn tons of liquid fuel—often a combination of liquid oxygen and liquid hydrogen. As the gases push out the bottom of the rocket, the ship rises. But you can launch a rocket with something as simple as air power.

FACTOID

In 1926, American scientist Robert Goddard launched the first liquid-fueled rocket. Thanks to his work and that of others, rockets now send astronauts, satellites, and probes into space.

What You Need

- A plastic tennis-ball can with lid or a plastic soda bottle with cap
- Three different types of soda straws: jumbo, super jumbo, and flexible
- Large pencil
- Scissors
- Tape
- Paper

What to Do

1 Poke a hole in the lid of the plastic can or bottle with a large pencil or the pointed end of a pair of scissors. (Ask an adult for help.)

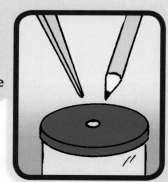

2 Cut the end of the flex straw on an angle. Push it through the hole in the lid or cap. The straw should fit snugly. Put the lid back on.

3 Stick a jumbo straw into the end of the flex straw. Tape it in place.

4 Make a rocket by folding over a half-inch of the end of a super-jumbo straw. (These straws can be found at a place that sells milk shakes.) Tape down the end.

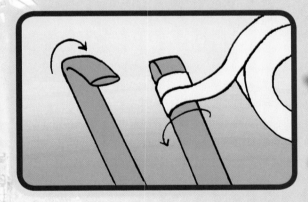

5 Make fins from paper to help your rocket fly straight. Tape on two or three paper fins to your super-jumbo straw.

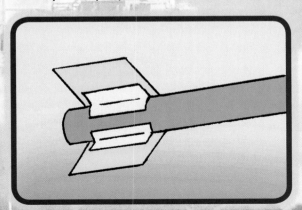

6 Slide the super-jumbo straw over the jumbo launcher straw. Aim and give the can or bottle a sharp squeeze. Watch it blast off.

Why It Works

Air pressure, not burning gases, makes your rocket take off. When you squeeze the can or bottle, the air inside the straw is compressed into a smaller space. This causes the pressure in the container to increase. To release the pressure, air rushes out the open end of the straw, causing it to fly up and away—just like a real rocket.

FACTOID

When a rocket reaches a height of 150 miles, it must reach a speed of nearly five miles per second to orbit Earth. If the rocket moves at a speed of seven miles per second or faster, it will reach escape velocity and head into outer space.

HOW Does the Stomach Digest Food?

If you gulp down too much pizza too fast, your stomach will expand. Nerve endings in your belly tell your brain, "You're full. Stop eating!" And you do—after having that one last slice. But what is happening to the pizza you've eaten?

The slices are taking a long journey through the digestive system. After you swallow, the food goes down a tube called the esophagus (es-*ahf*-a-gus). The pizza then makes a pit stop in the stomach. The stomach is a muscular bag that crushes the food and churns it in a strong acid until the pizza turns into a soup-like liquid called chyme (kym). The chyme sits in the stomach for hours, until it's ready to move on to the intestines and out the other end.

Check out how food gets broken down in the stomach and learn why the stomach doesn't digest itself).

Mucous cells: These cells produce mucus, a thick liquid that coats the stomach lining and keeps the hydrochloric acid from touching it. The cells also produce bicarbonate. When this chemical mixes with the mucus, it turns the acid into water. Even if the stomach does get damaged by the acid, every cell in the lining is replaced every week.

The human body is an amazing, complicated machine. It doesn't come with an instruction book, but we know a lot about how the parts work and how to keep them running.

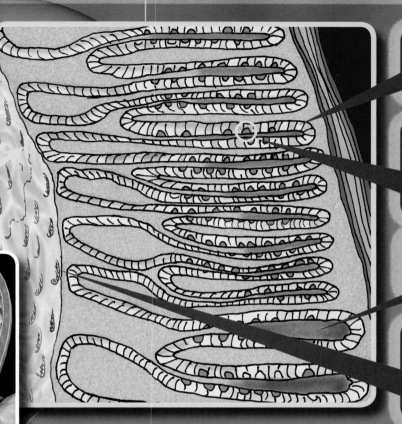

Pepsin cells: They produce a chemical called pepsin, which breaks down proteins and carbohydrates in food.

Acid cells: The hydrochloric acid made in acid cells turns food into liquid. Hydrochloric acid is strong enough to dissolve wood and even some metals. If too much of this is produced, it can irritate the stomach lining.

Gastric glands: Hydrochloric acid and pepsin mix in narrow tubes called gastric glands.

Gastric pits: The mix of hydrochloric acid and pepsin flows out of the gastric gland and into the stomach through millions of tiny holes called gastric pits.

The Poop on Poop

The solid waste that you flush down the toilet is made of a lot more than undigested food. What was once your meal is called feces (*fees*-ease). This is a mass of undigested food, dead cells that got scraped off the intestine walls, and lots of living and dead bacteria. The large intestine is full of bacteria that help digest food. When feces pass through the large intestine, they pick up the bacteria. About half the feces is made of this bacteria—they even give the feces its brown color.

When we eat something, a wave goes up and down the digestive system. This wave pushes the feces to the end of the large intestine and into a storage area for poop called the rectum. When the rectum fills with feces and stretches, sensory cells let the brain know that it's time to go to the bathroom. Muscles along the anus relax and allow the waste to exit the body.

HOW Do We Cry?

When you see a sad movie, you cry. When a piece of dust gets in your eye, you shed tears. Our eyes can turn into a water fountain pretty easily. Even when we're not crying, tears are constantly being produced. Every time we blink, we spread tears over our eyes. This type of tears is produced slowly and steadily. They keep our eyes smooth, clear, and free of bits of dust and pollen. Tears also keep our eyes healthy. They contain salt and proteins that nourish the eye, and a chemical called lysozyme (*lie*-suh-zyme) that fights germs.

If an eye gets irritated, the tear glands produce a flood of tears. This can happen when wind, smoke, or fumes strike our eyeballs. People also cry when they are sad, happy, or in pain. Tears produced by strong emotions contain hormones produced in the body. Crying washes away these hormones—and sometimes makes you feel better.

eye is the lacrimal (*lack*-re-mal), or tear, gland. It is about the size of an almond. This gland produces tears that constantly coat the eye. The tears flow through tiny ducts, or openings, onto the eyeball.

Eyelid: Every time the eyes blink, the lids push tears down toward the nose and into the lacrimal sac.

Eyeball: Tears flow across the eyeball, coating it like a film.

Nose: Tears drain from the lacrimal sac into the nose. When a person cries a lot, tears flow into the nose, so it seems like the person's nose is running.

Lacrimal sac: Tears drain out of the inner side of the eyes through small holes. They travel down into the lacrimal sac, which is located between the eye and the top of the nose.

Do Animals Have Emotions?

Humans aren't the only animals to shed tears. Most mammals have tear glands that work like ours to clean and keep eyes moist. But no one knows for sure if animals tear up from emotion. In fact, no one knows for sure if animals feel emotions. But more and more researchers are coming to believe they do.

Many scientists agree that animals feel pain, which is an emotion. But some animal experts believe they feel other emotions, as well. An experiment showed that rats feel bad when they see other rats suffering. Gorillas seem to act sad when their child dies. Mother elephants appear upset when separated from their offspring. There are many stories of a dog acting unhappy when its human owner dies. One researcher claims that birds feel many emotions and another scientist says that even fish feel fear. However, many scientists say there is no proof animals have emotions.

HOW Do Medicines Work?

When you're feeling sick, you might need to see a doctor. After you tell the doctor what's wrong, the doctor will examine you. He or she will look into your eyes, nose and throat, listen to your heartbeat and lungs, and take your blood pressure. Armed with information, the doctor will offer a diagnosis—the reason why you are sick—and give a treatment. Often that treatment is some kind of medicine.

Medicine is a chemical that comes in many forms. It can be a liquid, tablet, or capsule you swallow. Drugs can be injected with a needle right into the bloodstream. Creams or ointments are absorbed through the skin. Drops are made for the eyes or ears. Inhalers spray a drug into the nose or throat. Drugs can fight an illness, prevent an illness, and make the symptoms of an illness less strong.

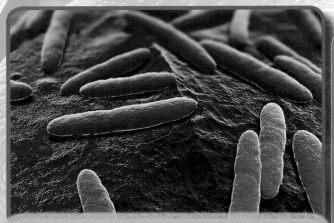

Disease Fighters: An antibiotic kills bacteria or keeps them from multiplying. Bacteria (shown here greatly magnified) are germs that can sometimes cause disease. Certain drugs also kill other types of microorganisms that can lead to disease, such as fungi and parasites. Medicine can also target cells that aren't working normally, such as cancer cells.

Be Prepared: A vaccine is made of a dead or weakened part of a germ, such as a flu virus. When a vaccine is injected into a person, the body reacts by building up defenses for that particular germ. If that type of germ one day tries to infect the person, the body will be ready to attack it right away.

FACTOID

Many medicines are based on substances found in nature. For example, antibiotics are often made from mold, fungi, and bacteria.

Perfect Timing

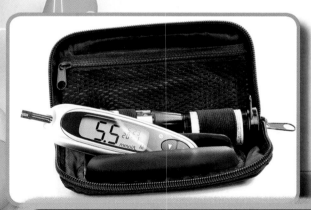

Pain Killers: Pain killers like aspirin can make you feel better while your body heals. If a part of the body is injured, nerve endings send pain signals to the brain. The drugs interfere with the message, so the pain stops.

Some medicines are solid pills. The medicine dissolves all at once inside the body. For other medicines, it's important that they release their medicine slowly, so the body doesn't absorb it all at once. These are called time-release drugs. They are usually capsules that hold hundreds of tiny hollow balls, or pellets. Inside each ball is the drug. Some balls have a thin coating. These dissolve within an hour or so after swallowing and release their

drug in the stomach. The drug goes through the stomach walls and into the bloodstream. Balls with thicker walls don't dissolve until hours later, after they reach the intestine. The medicine enters the bloodstream through the intestine walls. The balls are sometimes different colors, based on the thickness of the coating.

Replacements: Sometimes the body doesn't produce enough, or any, of a substance. Drugs can be used to replace those substances. For example, a person with a disease called diabetes needs extra insulin to stay healthy and gets it in an insulin shot. The shot comes in an insulin kit like the one in the photo.

FACTOID

The first drug sold in tablet form was aspirin, in 1899. The chemical in aspirin comes from a substance found in willow bark.

HOW Do Eyeglasses Help Us See Better?

The eye is an amazing and complicated organ that starts working when light passes through the cornea. This is a clear shield over the eye that focuses light. After the light enters a small opening called the pupil, the lens focuses it again, but this time onto the retina at the back of the eye, where an image appears upside down. The retina is covered by cells that are sensitive to light. When light hits the retina, the cells send electric signals to the brain. The brain unscrambles the signals to make the right-side-up image that we see.

We take vision for granted, but our eyes don't always work perfectly. Some people have trouble seeing near or far objects clearly. If things are blurry, glasses or contact lenses may be needed. When we put them on, the world comes back into focus.

DID YOU KNOW?

● Ancient Babylonians and Greeks tried to see more clearly by looking through pieces of rock quartz. The crystal acted like a lens and focused light.

● Benjamin Franklin invented the first bifocal lenses around 1760. These allowed a person to see clearly up close and at a distance through the same pair of eyeglasses.

The Eyes Have It

To make sure your eyes stay healthy, follow these tips.

○ Eat five servings of fruits and vegetables every day. Nutrients in foods such as oranges, broccoli, corn, carrots, and green, leafy vegetables will help keep your peepers perfect.

○ Get plenty of exercise. Physical activity gets the blood moving, which delivers more oxygen and nutrients to your eyes. But be sure to protect your eyes with goggles if you play contact sports.

○ When on the computer, look away for 20 seconds every 20 minutes to avoid eyestrain. Don't sit too close to the screen. Your eyes should be about two feet away.

○ Get an eye exam by a doctor at least once every two years.

Focus on the Eyes

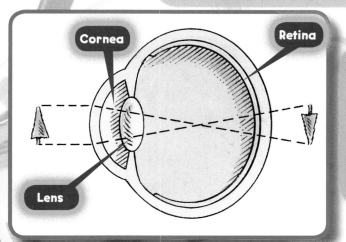

Farsighted: A farsighted person can see objects at a distance clearly. Things that are close look fuzzy because either the eyeball is too short or the cornea is too flat. Light from near objects focus behind the retina, not on it. Glasses or contact lenses that correct this are convex—or curve out slightly, which makes the light spread apart and focus on the retina.

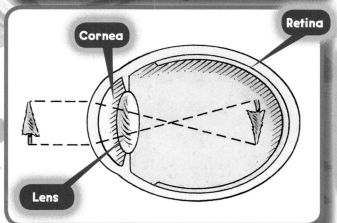

Nearsighted: Nearsighted people see close objects clearly. Objects that are far away are blurry because the eyeball is too long or the cornea curves too much. The light from distant objects focuses in front of the retina. Glasses or contact lenses that correct this are concave, meaning they curve in slightly. This makes the light bend in and focus on the retina.

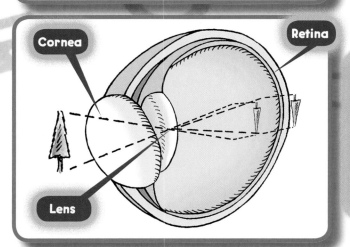

Astigmatism: A person with astigmatism (ah-*stig*-ma-tiz-im) may see objects both near and far out of focus. The cornea of most people is shaped like a baseball. With astigmatism, the cornea looks more like a football. Light scatters, focusing on different areas of the retina. This makes objects seem wavy. To correct this problem, glasses and contact lenses focus light on the same area of the retina.

HOW Does the Body Fight Germs?

Germs are all around us. Most are harmless, but a few can make us sick. When bacteria, viruses, and other microorganisms (tiny one-celled life forms) try to infect us, our immune system springs into action. To be immune is to be protected, and the immune system has several ways to fight germs and keep us healthy. The first line of defense is our skin, which keeps out germs. The natural openings in the body, such as the mouth and eyes, produce chemicals to kill germs. If germs do get through our outer defenses, they are attacked by different types of white blood cells.

When we are infected, we feel sick: glands in the neck or armpits get swollen and tender, our temperature rises, skin that is cut might get red and sore. These are signs that our body is battling the germs.

Chemicals in saliva and in tears fight bacteria.

The surface of the skin is full of dead cells, which don't give germs a foothold. The skin also produces chemicals that can kill some bacteria.

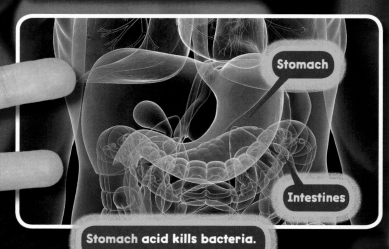

Stomach

Intestines

Stomach acid kills bacteria.

Mucus in the nose can trap germs.

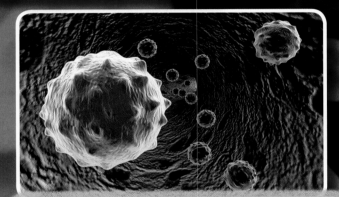

White blood cells, including macrophages (*mac-roh-faj-ez*), are in different organs and also travel through fluid in the lymph (limf) system and in the blood. They patrol the body looking for germs to swallow and kill. These cells are so small, they can only be seen through powerful microscopes.

Keep Healthy

The immune system works hard to fight off germs and keep you healthy. But there are ways you can pitch in and help out your body's defenses.

● **Get enough sleep.** You should be getting 9 to 10 hours of sleep every night.

● **Eat right.** Try to eat three regular meals of nutritious foods that include fruits, vegetables, and whole grains. Avoid sugary foods and drinks, as well as fast foods. Drink plenty of water.

● **Exercise.** When you exercise, you strengthen your bones, muscles, and heart, and make the lungs work better. Being active burns off extra fat, and it helps you digest food. Do anything that makes you move—even walking is good for you and your body.

● **Reduce stress.** Too much stress over a long period of time can weaken the immune system. Talk over your problems with your parents or teachers. To reduce stress, exercise, enjoy hobbies, read for pleasure, or play with a pet.

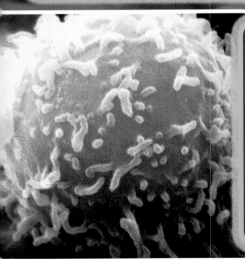

Shown here is a photo taken by an electron microscope of a special type of white blood cell called a lymphocyte (*lim*-foh-site). Some lymphocytes produce proteins called antibodies. The antibodies stick on germs, so other white blood cells know to kill them.

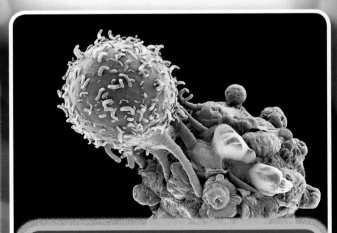

This computer-generated image shows a white blood cell called a killer lymphocyte (the ball on the left). As it travels through the body, it searches out and attacks cancer cells (shown on the right), as well as germs hiding in cells.

HOW Does Loud Music Hurt Your Hearing?

How the Ear Works

You've probably heard that listening to iPods and MP3 players through earbuds at high volume can hurt your hearing. Unfortunately, people who hear the warnings don't always turn down the volume. Some people think the maximum setting on an iPod is safe. But at the highest volume, some music players are as loud as a chainsaw or rock concert.

Researchers have found that listening with earbuds or in-ear headphones to music at full blast for just five minutes a day can, over time, cause permanent hearing loss. Listening at a high volume an hour a day can damage your hearing after five years. So when you're listening to music, turn down the volume.

Auditory canal: Sound enters through the auditory canal and is funneled to the eardrum.

Eardrum: Sound makes the eardrum vibrate back and forth like a drum.

FACTOID

The tiny bones of the middle ear—the hammer, anvil, and stirrup—are the smallest bones in the body. They stay the same size throughout a person's lifetime.

Ossicles: The vibrating eardrum shakes three ossicles (*ah*-sic-uls), or tiny bones. Because of the way they look, they are called the hammer, anvil, and stirrup. As they move, they push and pull a membrane at the beginning of the inner ear.

Inner ear: This contains the cochlea, as well as the semicircular canals—the part of the ear that controls balance.

Nerves: They carry electrical signals to the brain.

Cochlea: The cochlea (*koh*-klee-ah) is filled with a fluid that vibrates when the ossicles vibrate. Those vibrations reach an area that contains 15,000 to 20,000 tiny hairs. The fluid makes the hairs bend. As they bend, they send electrical signals through nerves to the brain. The brain "hears" the signals as sound. Loud noise can damage or kill hair cells, and that causes hearing loss. Once the hairs die, they don't grow back.

Sound Advice

This chart shows how many decibels different sounds produce. A decibel is a measure of a sound's loudness. Any sound above 90 decibels can, over time, damage a person's hearing.

Sound	Decibels (db)
Lowest sound that can be heard	0
Breathing	10
Mosquito	20
Whisper	30
Refrigerator hum	40
Normal conversation	50-65
Laughter	60
Vacuum cleaner, hair dryer	70
Motorcycle	90
Train, garbage truck	100
Snowmobile, jet overhead at 100 feet	105
Drill, jackhammer	105
Jet taking off	130
Rock concert	140

HOW to Make a Stethoscope

Lub-dub, lub-dub, lub-dub. That's the sound a doctor hears when she listens to your heart through a stethoscope. The heart has four flaps of skin, or valves, that open and close as blood pumps through them. The lub-dub sound of a heartbeat is actually the noise the valves make when they open and close. You can hear the sounds if you put your ear to someone's chest. But a stethoscope makes the sound much clearer.

On one end of a stethoscope is a plastic disk, or diaphragm (*die*-a-fram), which is pressed against a person's skin over the heart. Sounds make the diaphragm vibrate. The sound waves travel up two tubes, through the earpieces, and into the doctor's ears. A doctor uses the stethoscope to hear if the heart is beating normally. If you want to hear what your doctor hears, make your own stethoscope.

DID YOU KNOW?

The human heart beats about 100,000 times during one day, 35 million times a year, and about 2.5 billion times in a lifetime.

What You Need

- 2 small funnels
- Rubber or plastic tubing (a cut up piece of garden hose, for example)
- Tape or glue
- Scissors
- Rubber band
- Balloon
- Timer

What to Do

1 Fit the rubber tubing into each end of the two funnels. Tape the tube tight to the funnel.

2 Blow up the balloon in order to stretch it out and then let the air out.

3 Cut off the balloon about one-third of the way up from the opening. Throw away the part with the opening.

4 Take the balloon and stretch it over the wide opening of one of the funnels. It should fit tightly. Hold it in place with a rubber band if the balloon slips off the funnel. You can use the stethoscope without a balloon, but the balloon makes it easier to pick up sounds.

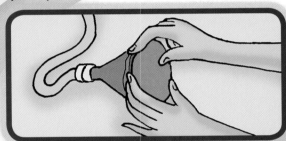

5 If you can't find one or two funnels or tubing, make your own. To make the funnel, cut out a six inch by six inch square of paper. Cut off one corner along a curved line. Roll the paper into a tube and tape it closed.

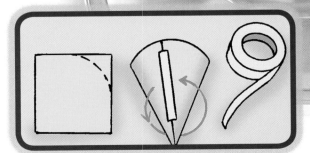

6 To make tubing, roll up a long piece of paper into a tube shape. Cut a piece off the tip of the funnel large enough to fit the tube. Tape the tube to the funnel.

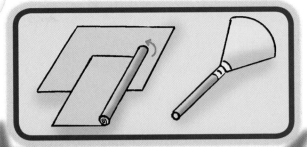

How to Use It

1. Feel your heartbeat with your hand. Your heart is located slightly to the left of the center of your chest.

2. Place the end of the funnel with the balloon (if you used one) over your heart. The funnel should touch your skin.

3. Put the other end of the funnel up to your ear. Listen for a soft beating sound. Count the number of beats you hear in 20 seconds. Multiply that number by three to calculate the number of beats your heart makes in one minute.

4. Run for a few minutes or do some other exercise and then listen to your heart again. Compare the results.

HOW to Find Your Dominant Eye

About 90 percent of people write, eat, and throw with their right hand. That means their right side is dominant, or in control. About 10 percent of people are dominant on their left side. Some people use their right and left hands equally. They are ambidextrous (am-bee-*dex*-trus). Some researchers think people have a dominant side because one side of the brain may be more dominant than the other side. But no one knows for sure why people are righties or lefties.

The hand isn't the only part of the body that can be dominant. To find out which foot is dominant, check out which foot a person kicks a ball with. Or which foot a person lifts first when climbing stairs or puts down when stepping on something. An ear can also be dominant. It's usually the ear a person uses to listen on a phone. Even an eye can be dominant. To find out which one of your eyes is dominant, try this experiment.

What to Do

1 Put your arms straight out in front of you. Your palms should face forward.

2 Make a triangle by overlapping your fingers and thumbs. Bring your hands closer together until there is a small opening, about the size of a quarter. You should be able to see through the triangle with just one eye.

3 With your arms held straight out, look at a small object in your room or an object in the distance through the opening you made with your hands. Stare at it with both eyes open.

4 Keeping both eyes open, slowly move the triangle back toward your face. As you do this, make sure the object is still in the opening. When the triangle nearly touches your face, note which eye it is in front of. That is your dominant eye.

5 If you want to double-check that you've found your dominant eye, try this: Look at the object again through the little triangle made by your hands. Keep your hands and head still. Close your right eye. If you can still see the object through the triangle, it means your left eye is dominant.

6 Now open your right eye and close your left eye. If you only see your hand, but no opening, your right eye is dominant.

Left Is Right

Since right-handers outnumber left-handers, lefties might feel a little, well, left out. Living in a right-handed world can be challenging for left-handers. It's harder to press the buttons on a watch worn on the right wrist. Remote controls and microwave controls are placed for righties. Most scissors are hard for lefties to use, and CD cases are difficult to open. But you have to hand it to lefties: Many of them have gone on to greatness. Here is just a (left) handful of famous left-handed people.

- Bill Clinton
- Ronald Reagan
- John McCain
- Alexander the Great
- Henry Ford
- Bill Gates
- Barack Obama
- Bart Simpson and his creator, Matt Groening
- Leonardo da Vinci
- Angelina Jolie
- Eminem
- Cliff Lee
- Isaac Newton
- Helen Keller
- Babe Ruth

HOW Are Computers and Other Electronics Recycled?

Many people know how to recycle plastic, glass, metal, and paper products. But how do we get rid of computers, cell phones, TVs, and other electronic devices that we don't want?

What should people do with them when they want to get rid of the machines? One solution is to give away useable electronics to schools, charities, and other groups. If the device can't be reused, it can be recycled.

See how a large recycling plant takes gadgets apart and puts some back together.

Every day, recycling plants receive **electronic waste (e-waste)**, including cell phones, computers, cameras, and printers.

E-waste that can't be broken apart by workers is fed into machines that separate out pieces made of different materials, such as **copper**. Many electronics contain small amounts of valuable metals, such as gold, which are removed and sold. Dangerous materials, such as lead, are also removed and sent to special landfills and waste plants.

It's important to protect the environment. This chapter shows some ways we can reduce energy use and save our natural resources.

Workers stack discarded computers that will be stripped of their parts.

Computer monitors are taken apart. The pieces from these and other gadgets are stored according to what they are made of. As many of the parts as possible are recycled—from plastic wrapping to broken glass and metal scraps. These are sold to separate recycling factories.

Much e-waste contains parts, such as circuits, that will be sold to manufacturers and used again in new products or in rebuilt devices.

DID YOU KNOW?

○ About 7,500 pounds of gold can be recovered from 100 million recycled cell phones.

○ The U.S. government has a website that lists e-waste recycling information: http://www.epa.gov/osw/conserve/materials/ecycling/donate.htm.

HOW Can You Make Your House Greener?

Going green means trying to reduce pollution and preserve natural resources. People can go green at school, at work, and especially at home. From the materials used in its construction to where the windows are placed, there are many ways to make a green building. One way is to build it with materials that don't harm the people inside or the environment. Another way is to make sure the building doesn't use a lot of energy for heating or cooling. Eco-friendly buildings are often powered by sustainable resources such as sunlight. Green builders also try to recycle and reuse materials in their buildings.

Going green can save money on energy bills and be better for the health of people—and the health of the planet. Check out some ways to help make a home more friendly to the environment.

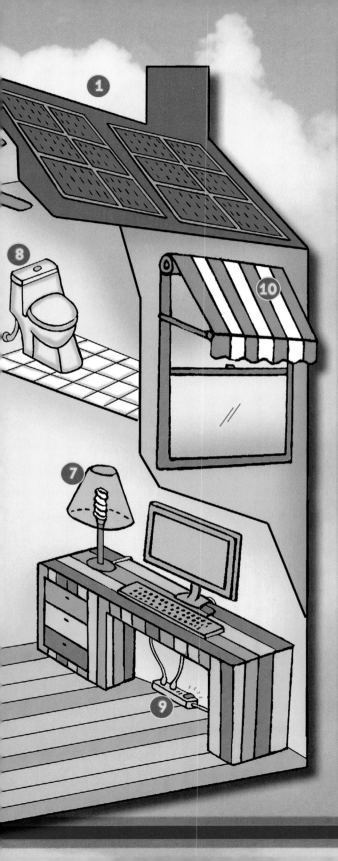

1. Solar panels on the roof can generate electricity from sunlight.

2. Bring plants into the house that remove pollutants from the air. Two of these are English ivy and spider plants.

3. A thermostat can be programmed to keep a house cooler in the winter and warmer in the summer. This saves energy.

4. Floors and furniture can be made from reused wood, which is wood recycled from old buildings or thrown-out furniture. Use wood, such as bamboo, that doesn't come from endangered forests.

5. Use cloth towels and napkins instead of ones made from paper.

6. Use slow-flow faucets in the kitchen and bathroom. They reduce the amount of water used for washing and showering.

7. Replace regular incandescent light bulbs with compact fluorescent bulbs to save electricity.

8. New toilets cut down the amount of water used for each flush.

9. When computers and other electronics are turned off, they still use power. Connect them to a power strip that you can turn off to stop the drain of electricity. Or just unplug the items when not in use.

10. Plant shade trees and put up awnings or shades to keep sunlight from making the house too warm. Inside, cool off with fans instead of air conditioners.

11. To reduce energy use, insulate the walls to keep heat and cold from escaping outside.

12. Fill in the openings around doors and windows to keep out the weather.

13. All new appliances should have an Energy Star label on them, especially the fridge, which uses a great amount of energy. Products with these labels use less electricity than older models.

HOW Do Wind Turbines Make Electricity?

Wind can sometimes be a destructive force. But wind is also a great help to humans. Over the centuries, windmills have been used to pump water, drain lakes, cut wood, and grind grain. Today, a kind of windmill is being used to produce electricity. Called wind turbines, these machines make in one year only a little over one percent of the total electricity generated in the U.S. Still, this is enough to power the entire state of Colorado.

The amount of electricity generated by wind has been growing over the last few years. One big reason is that wind is renewable energy, which means it will never run out. Also, wind turbines don't cause pollution, are cheap to run, and don't take up much space compared to the energy they produce. Some people think the answer to our energy problems is blowing in the wind.

FACTOID

The largest wind turbine blade in the world is 200 feet long. The diameter of two spinning blades is greater than the length of a football field, including the end zones.

Wind makes the lightweight blades turn. The faster the blades spin, the more electricity is produced. The blades are connected to the drive shaft.

As the blades turn, the drive shaft spins. The drive shaft is connected to the gears.

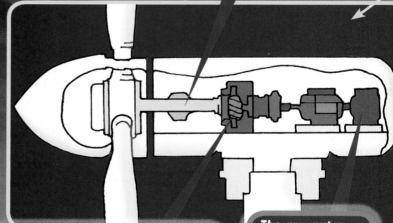

The drive shaft turns gears, which make another drive shaft spin even faster. This drive shaft leads to a generator.

The generator changes the spin of the drive shaft into an electrical current.

Wind turbines are built tall to catch winds that often blow high above the ground. Most are as tall as a 20-story building, while some are twice that tall.

The **casing** holds the drive shaft, gears, and a generator.

Electricity from the generator flows down wires to a **transformer**. This device makes the current stronger. The electricity is sent through power lines to homes and towns.

Ill Winds?

Not everyone loves wind power. Some people complain that the huge machines make the landscape ugly. Wind turbines also make a steady noise, which bothers some people. Some environmentalists oppose wind turbines because they believe the spinning blades sometimes kill birds and bats.

Those in favor of wind turbines say the machines help the environment. Wind turbines are a clean source of energy and will reduce the use of polluting fossil fuels, such as coal and gas. The controversy continues to swirl.

TOP 5 Wind-Power-Producing States

1. Texas
2. Iowa
3. California
4. Minnesota
5. Washington

Source: U.S. Energy Information Administration

FACTOID

Wind farms are large groups of wind turbines. The world's largest wind farm is the Horse Hollow Wind Energy Center in Texas. Its 421 wind turbines produce enough energy to power 220,000 homes for a year.

HOW to Make a Landfill

Every year, the average American throws away about 1,600 pounds of garbage. About 54 percent of all trash in the U.S. goes into landfills—large areas of land in which waste material is buried. About 15 percent of trash is burned in incinerators to produce energy. The rest of the trash is recycled.

Landfills are designed to prevent dangerous waste from escaping into the soil and getting into the water supply. A thick layer of clay or plastic separates the garbage from the ground. Every day, workers add a layer of soil to cover the trash on top. But just because garbage is at a dump doesn't mean it disappears. Many materials don't decompose, or break down, very quickly. To see what does and doesn't decompose in a landfill, try this experiment.

What You Need

- Rubber gloves
- A medium- or large-size clay flowerpot
- A small stone
- Some soil
- Food scraps, leaves, non-glossy paper, polystyrene foam, plastic sandwich bags, aluminum foil
- Water
- 2 glass plates
- Newspapers

What to Do

1 Put the stone over the hole at the bottom of the flowerpot. This will keep water from draining out of the hole too quickly.

2 Fill one-third of the flowerpot with soil.

3 Tear up the garbage (the food scraps, leaves, and so on) into small pieces. Place the pieces on top of the soil in the flowerpot.

4 Cover the garbage with another layer of soil. The soil should just about fill the flowerpot. Pour just enough water into the flowerpot so it's completely damp, but not soaking wet.

5 Cover the top of the flowerpot with the glass plate. Put the other plate under the flowerpot so water and soil won't leak out the bottom.

6 Put the flowerpot in a warm, dark place, such as under the kitchen sink. Check every few days. Add more water to keep the soil damp.

7 At the end of one month, take out the flowerpot and empty it on a large piece of newspaper. (Get your parent's okay first.) Put on rubber gloves and spread out the soil so you can see the condition of the garbage.

What Happened

The food, paper, and leaves should have broken down into a soft material. This happens when bacteria in the soil feed on organic, or living, materials. The plastic, foam, and foil are not organic. Bacteria can't break them down.

Air and water in the flowerpot allow bacteria to live. In a landfill, layers of soil and trash press down so tightly, water and air can't get in. Bacteria can't survive, so even organic materials such as paper don't break down easily.

HOW to Make Recycled Paper

Paper was probably invented in China in 105 A.D. Before then, people wrote on anything that was handy, from cave walls and wet clay to animal skins and plants. True paper is made from tiny plant fibers, such as cotton or wood, that have been softened and pressed into thin sheets.

The U.S. uses about 85 million tons of paper and paper products each year. The good news is that about half of these products, which include money, bandages, egg cartons, and masking tape, are made from recycled paper. The more paper that's recycled, the less paper that ends up in a dump. Recycling also saves trees and the water used to make paper. So help the environment—and have fun—by making new paper from old.

What You Need

- 6 or 7 sheets of newspaper
- Glass bowl
- Cornstarch
- Hot water
- Measuring spoon
- Aluminum foil
- Wooden spoon
- Kitchen strainer
- Scissors
- Sharpened pencil
- Sponge

What to Do

1 Cut and tear four or five sheets of newspaper into the smallest pieces you can.

2 Put the shredded paper into the bowl and cover with hot water. Mix the paper in the water with a spoon. Let it stand for several hours, stirring once in a while.

3 When the paper looks very mushy, put one or two tablespoons of cornstarch into the bowl, add more hot water, and stir again with the spoon.

4 Fold a sheet of aluminum foil into the size of the sheet of paper you want to make. Poke several dozen small holes in the foil with the sharpened pencil. Put it aside for later use.

5 Using a spoon or ladle, transfer the softened paper from the bowl into the strainer and let the water drain.

6 Tear off another sheet of aluminum foil that's a little larger than the size of the page you want to make. Place the foil on the remaining sheets of newspaper. With a spoon, transfer the pulpy paper from the strainer to the sheet of foil. Spread it out on the foil in any shape you wish your page to look like.

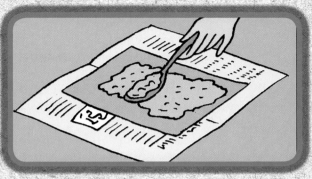

7 Put the aluminum foil with holes on top of the paper and press down on it. Sponge off any water that comes through the holes. Remove the top sheet of foil. If there are any holes in the paper, pinch them together with your fingers.

8 Place another sheet of foil on top of the paper. Put a book as large as the paper on top of the foil and press down to flatten the paper. Remove the book and top foil and let the paper dry overnight. When the paper is dry, carefully peel it off the bottom sheet of foil. You can leave the edges of the paper rough or trim them with scissors. Grab a pen and see if you have the write stuff!

Glossary

abdomen the part of the body that contains the organs needed for digestion

afterimage an image that a person continues to see even after what caused the image is no longer there

ambidextrous able to use both hands equally well

Antarctica the ice-covered continent around the South Pole

antenna a metal device used for sending and receiving radio waves

antibiotic a medicine that kills bacteria

antibodies proteins in the body that fight off disease and infection

Arctic the area around the North Pole

asteroid rocks, some the size of small planets, that orbit between Mars and Jupiter

astigmatism the inability of the eye to focus light because the cornea doesn't curve normally

avalanche a large mass of snow and ice that falls down the side of a mountain

axis a straight line around which an object turns

bacteria microscopic single-celled organisms found in water, air, and soil

baking soda a substance that gives off carbon dioxide, which causes dough to rise

baking powder a substance made of baking soda and an acidic powder that gives off carbon dioxide, causing dough to rise

battery a device that produces an electrical current

black powder a substance, also known as gunpowder, that causes an explosion

blubber a thick layer of fat found in marine animals that protects, or insulates, them against the cold

borax powder powder or crystals used to clean clothes

bower a shelter made of plants

buoyancy the ability of an object to float or rise when submerged in a liquid

burr the rough, prickly outside of a fruit

burrow a hole or tunnel dug by a small animal and used as a home or a place of safety

calve to break off, as when icebergs calve from a glacier

canal a human-made waterway used for travel, to ship goods, or to irrigate land

canyon a deep valley with steep sides, often formed by a river

capsaicin a chemical making chili peppers taste hot

cells the basic structure of all living things; in a beehive, six-sided structures made of beeswax that store food and house growing bees

centrifugal force the force directed away from the center of a revolving body

chyme food that has been turned into a liquid-like mass in the stomach

cacao the seeds from a cacao tree that are used to make chocolate

comet a large chunk of rock surrounded by frozen gas and ice that orbits the sun

condensation the changing of gas into a liquid

cones cells in the retina of an eye that detect color

constellation a group of stars that seem to form a pattern in the sky

cornea the clear area that covers the front of the eye and focuses light

crystal a substance formed when atoms or molecules are arranged in a pattern that repeats

decibel a unit used to measure loudness

decompose the process by which a dead organism rots away

derailer (derailleur) a device on a bicycle that shifts gears by moving a chain from one gear wheel to another

diaphragm a thin disk that vibrates and produces sound waves

dissolve to mix a solid substance with a liquid until it is included in the liquid

distilled water water that has been boiled and condensed to remove any salts or minerals

e-waste electronic waste, such as computers or cell phones, that is thrown away

earthquake a trembling movement of Earth's crust that can damage buildings and other structures

electromagnetic field a magnetic field produced when electricity flows through a wire

electron a tiny particle that moves around the nucleus of an atom

electroreceptor a special sensory organ in sharks and some other fish that detects electricity given off by other sea creatures

endangered a species, or type of living thing, that is in immediate danger of becoming extinct, or dying out completely

entomologist a scientist who studies insects

equator an imaginary line that circles a planet at equal distance from its two poles

esophagus the tube that passes food from the mouth to the stomach

evaporate to change a liquid into a gas, or vapor

exoplanet a planet outside our solar system

extinct the dying out of a species of living things

farsighted an inability to see close objects clearly

fossil part of a plant or animal from the distant past that has been preserved in the Earth's crust

friction the force that one surface exerts on another when the two rub against each other

fungus a type of organism, including yeast, molds, and mushrooms, that is neither a plant nor animal

gear a wheel with teeth that turns another wheel with teeth, so the motion of one controls the speed of the other

generator a machine that changes mechanical energy into electrical energy, often by moving a copper wire through a magnetic field

glacier a large mass of ice and snow that has been pressed down over thousands of years and which slowly moves forward

gland a cell or group of cells that produce a substance that a body uses or gets rid of

gluten a protein in wheat and other grains that makes dough elastic when it is kneaded

gravity the force of attraction between two objects

greenhouse gas a gas, such as carbon dioxide and methane, that helps cause global warming

hibernate to spend the winter resting or sleeping in order to save energy

hive a structure that houses a colony of bees

hurricane a storm that forms over tropical waters with winds that reach at least 74 miles per hour

honeycomb a group of cells made of beeswax in a beehive

hybrid something that combines two or more different things, such as a car that runs on electricity and gas

iceberg a large chunk of ice that breaks off from a glacier or an ice shelf and floats in the water

immune system cells, proteins, and tissue that protect the body from infection and disease

infection the invasion of the body by a microorganism, such as a virus, that causes disease

inflammation pain, swelling, or redness in the body caused by infection or an injury

infrared radiation electromagnetic waves that can't be seen by the human eye but can be sensed as heat

insulator a substance that doesn't allow heat or electricity to pass through it

joint the part of the body where two bones are connected

kernel the inner, soft part of a seed or grain, which can be eaten

kinetic energy the energy of movement

landfill a site designed so large amounts of trash can be buried safely

larva the earliest stage of an animal, just after it has hatched and before it changes into an adult

leaven a substance, such as yeast, that causes dough to rise

lens the part of the eye that helps bring rays of light into focus

ligament tough tissue that connects two bones

lightning a bright flash of light caused by electricity flowing from one part of a cloud to another or from a cloud to the surface of the Earth

limestone a kind of rock often used as a building material

liquid hydrogen hydrogen gas that has been cooled down into a liquid; it is used as rocket fuel

lock a large chamber with gates at each end that fills with water to raise ships and empties water to lower ships as they pass through it

lymph system the tissues and organs that produce and carry cells that fight infections

magnetic field the lines of force created by and surrounding the sun and the planets

magnet an object that attracts or repels other magnets and attracts certain kinds of metal, such as iron and nickel

magnetosphere the magnetic field that surrounds a planet and which extends far into outer space

mammal a warm-blooded animal with a backbone that has hair or fur and feeds milk to their young

mass extinction an extinction caused by a widespread disaster that kills off many species of living things in a fairly short period of time

membrane a thin layer of tissue that covers, separates, or connects areas of the body

microphage white blood cells that play a role in the immune system by killing bacteria and other cells that enter the body

microwave electromagnetic radiation, similar to radio waves, that is used in microwave ovens to cook food

mineral a substance that occurs naturally and is found in rocks

molecule the smallest part of a substance, made up of one or more atoms

mucus a thick fluid that coats and protects the nose, throat, lungs, and other areas of the body

nearsighted an inability to see objects in the distance clearly

nectar sweet liquid given off by a plant that attracts insects or birds, causing them to pollinate the plant

nocturnal active at night

nuclear reactor a device that uses radioactive materials to produce heat, which generates electrical power

oblong a rectangle that has one side longer than the others

orbit the path one body takes around another, such as the path of the Earth around the sun

paleontologist a scientist who studies fossils of prehistoric organisms

pentagonal a shape that has five sides and five angles inside the shape

pepsin a chemical produced in the stomach that helps break down proteins for digestion

pharaoh a king of ancient Egypt

photon a small particle of energy that all forms of electromagnetic radiation are made of

plankton tiny organisms that float in the sea and serve as food for fish

plaster a powder that becomes a paste when mixed with water and hardens as it dries

pollen a powdery substance produced by a flower and used to fertilize another flower

pollinate to fertilize a plant by transferring pollen grains from the male part of a plant to the female part of a plant

pollution the contamination of air, water, or soil by harmful substances

potential energy stored energy

power surge a sudden, unexpected increase in electricity that can damage computers and other electrical equipment

prey an animal that is hunted by another animal

primate a mammal that has such features as a large brain, five digits on their hands and feet; monkeys, apes, and humans are primates

prism a solid object with all flat sides and with ends that have the same shape

propeller spinning blades that make a boat, submarine, or airplane move

protein a substance basic to living cells and necessary for an organism to function; it is an important source of energy in a person's diet

pupa the stage in the development of certain insects that comes after the larva stage and before the adult stage; a pupa often changes into an adult while inside a cocoon or a hard outer layer

pupil the opening in the center of the eye through which light enters

pyrotechnician an expert in the use of fireworks

quarry an open area from which stones used for building things, such as limestone, are removed

radiation electromagnetic energy that moves in the form of waves

rain forest a dense forest that grows in warm or tropical regions where it rains heavily throughout the year

rectum the lower part of the large intestine

recycle to collect materials, such as metal cans and glass bottles, that have been thrown away in order to reuse them in new products

refrigerant a substance used in a refrigerator or air conditioner that lowers temperatures by absorbing heat

retina light-sensitive tissue located at the back of the eyeball

rodent a small mammal, such as a rat or beaver, with sharp front teeth used to chew

rods cells in the retina that are sensitive to black and white light

saturate to dissolve a substance in a liquid until no more can be dissolved

scent glands a special gland in mammals that produces a strong odor

seed the part of a plant that can grow into a new plant

solar panel a device made up of solar cells, which change sunlight into electricity

solution a uniform mixture formed when one substance is completely dissolved in another substance

sonar a method or device that locates objects by sending out sound waves and detecting the waves that bounce off the objects

species a group of similar organisms

spinneret a tube at the rear end of a spider, out of which comes silk in the form of a thread, which is used to spin webs

starch a carbohydrate that is produced in fruits and vegetables and is used as a source of energy by plants and animals

static electricity electricity produced when two objects touch and separate

storm surge water that is pushed toward the shore by strong winds, often caused by hurricanes as they move near land

suspension bridge a bridge whose roadway is suspended by cables attached to large towers at both ends

tapetum a layer of cells in the back of the eyes of certain animals that reflect light, making it easier to see in dim light

tendon tissue that connects bone to muscle

terrarium a glass container where plants or small animals, such as turtles, are raised and displayed

territory an area that an animal or group of animals live in and defend against other animals, especially those of the same species

thermostat a device that controls the temperature in a room or an entire house

threatened a species that is likely to become endangered in the future

tornado a dark, funnel-shaped cloud made of fast-spinning air

toxin a poisonous substance produced by plants, animals, and bacteria

ultraviolet radiation electromagnetic waves invisible to the human eye that can damage human cells

vaccine a medicine made of dead or weakened germs that prevents a person from getting sick from that germ

vapor a gas; also, tiny but visible particles that float in the air, such as smoke and steam

venom a poisonous substance produced by certain snakes and insects, usually given off in a bite or sting

virus a tiny particle that can cause different types of illnesses by entering a person's body through the nose, mouth, or breaks in the skin

viscosity the ability of a fluid to flow or not flow easily because of its thickness

volt a measurement of how much force there is in an electric circuit

wind turbine a machine that turns the power of the wind into electrical energy

yeast a one-celled fungus that gives off carbon dioxide

Index

A

absolute zero, 119
absorbers, 82
acid rain, 14
Africa, 94, 132
airplanes
    in astronaut training, 146
    how to make a paper, 108-109
    jet-powered, 108
    strangest, 109
Alexander the Great, 171
alligators, 15
Alps, 102
Amazon rain forest, 94
ambidextrous people, 170
American Red Cross, 42
animals
    affected by oil spills, 83-85
    architects, 23
    color change in, 10-11
    communication in, 6-7
    emotions in, 159
    guide, 39
    in frigid temperatures, 25
    marking territory, 26-27
    nocturnal, 16-17
    venomous, 13
Antarctica, 119
archaeological dig
    finding and removing fossils, 80-81
Arctic cod, 25
Arctic fox, 25
Arctic, the, 119
Arenas, Gilbert, 63
Arizona, 74
Asia, 94, 132
aspirin, 160-161
asteroids
    locating and tracking, 142
    nuclear blasts, 143
    striking Earth, 142
astigmatism, 163
astronauts
    in rockets, 154
    in simulators, 147
    in zero gravity conditions, 146-147
    mission specialists, 146
    requirements to become, 146
    training, 146-147
Atlanta, GA, 123
Atlantic Ocean, 29, 72, 93
Austin, TX, 123
Australia, 135

B

bacteria
    in food, 118
    in the large intestine, 157
    in the soil, 179
    in yogurt, 141
    infecting the body, 164
baking powder, 131
baking soda, 131
baking soda boat
    how to make, 106-107
ball
    baseball, 46, 64-65
    how to make a high-bounce, 64-65
    kinetic energy, 64
    Super Ball, 64-65
ballast tanks, 98
baseball
    bats, 46-47
    injuries in, 59
    Louisville Slugger Museum & Factory, 67
baseball bats
    billets, 47
    corking, 66
    Hillerich & Bradsby, 46
    how they are made, 46-47
    how to find the sweet spot, 66-67
    Louisville Slugger, 46-47
    metal, 67
    player's signature on, 47
    types of, 46
    vibrations in, 66
basketball
    court, 60-61
    injuries in, 59
bats
    gray, 15
    high-pitched sounds in, 17
    nocturnal vision in, 17
batteries
    in a survival kit, 43
    in hybrid cars, 100-101
    in smoke alarms, 34
bears
    Louisiana black, 15
    panda, 26
    polar, 24-25
beavers
    how they build dams, 22-23
    lodge, 22-23
    pond, 22
Belgium, 135
bergy bits, 92
bicycle
    parts of, 44-45
    gears, 44-45
birds
    cleaned after oil spills, 84-85
    emotions in, 159
    spreading chilies seeds, 136
blubber
    how to make, 24-25
    in marine mammals, 24
    in polar bears, 24
    thickness of, 24
blue whale
    blubber in, 24
    endangered, 7
    low- and high-pitched sounds, 7
    songs, 7
Bobcats, 61
bones (animal), 80-81
booms, 82
Borglum, Gutzon, 70
Boston Bruins, 60
bowerbird, 23
box jelly fish, 13
Brazil, 132
bread
    how it rises, 130-131
    in history, 130
    ingredients of, 131
    types of, 130-131
    yeast in, 130
bridge
    George Washington, 75
    Golden Gate, 75
    how to build a spaghetti bridge, 74-75
    Mackinac, 75
    Mike O'Callaghan-Pat Tillman
        Memorial, 73-74
    Tacoma Narrows, 75
    types of, 76
    Verrazano-Narrows, 75
Brihadeeswara Temple, 69
Burchett, M.J., 53
burdock plant, 117

C

cacao tree
    cacao beans, 132
    pods in, 132
caddisfly, 23
Cairo, 68, 69
California, 56, 60, 75, 123, 177
camera
    digital, 125
    features of, 125
    how to make your own, 124-125
    obscura, 124
capsaicin, 136-137
capstone, 69
capuchin monkeys, 39
car
    electric, 101
    hybrid, 100-101
carbon dioxide
    in baking soda and vinegar, 107
    in rain forests, 95
    in yeast, 131
cats
    as guide animals, 39
    how they mark their territory, 27
Central America, 72, 94
chameleons
    color change in, 10
    melanin, 10
    pigment cells, 10
    skin layers, 10
    types of, 10

Channel England-France, 103
Chicago, IL, 123
Children's Disaster Response, 42
chili pepper
    capsaicin in, 136-137
    parts of, 136-137
China, 105, 108, 154
chocolate
    cacao beans, 132
    cacao tree, 132
    conch machine, 133
    factory, 132
    hulling machine, 132
    in ice cream, 134
    liquor, 133
    milk in, 133
    nibs, 133
    paste, 133
clouds
    in Jupiter, 145
    in storms, 30, 36-37
color
    change in animals, 11
    complimentary, 89
    contrast, 89
    in icebergs, 93
Colorado River, 74-75
Colorado, 80
comets, 142
compass
    as a navigation tool, 40
    how to make, 40
compost, 115
computers
    desktop, 122
    hard drive in, 120
    in motion capture technology, 63
    laptop, 122
    safe surfing in Internet, 121
    viruses, 120-121
    wireless, 123
constellations
    Big Dipper, 153
    in ancient times, 153
    Orion, 153
contact lenses, 162-163
copper, 172
cornea
    in animals, 16
    in humans, 162-163
crochet, 117
crocodiles, 15
crystals
    as form of minerals, 97
    how to grow, 96-97
    shapes of, 96
    types of, 96
    underground caves, 96

D

Dalmatians, 35
dam,
    beaver, 22-23
    Hoover, 74

da Vinci, Leonardo, 171
De Mestral, George, 117
Denmark, 135
diagnosis, 168
diamond
    crystals, 96
    in Mohs scale list, 97
Dinosaur National Monument, 80
dinosaurs
    possible reasons for extinction, 14-15
dogs
    as service, 38-39
    how they mark their territory, 27
dominant
    ear, 170
    eye, 170-171
    foot, 170

E

ear
    parts of, 166-167
Earth
    and Jupiter, 145
    and the sun, 148,150
    axis of, 54
    dinosaurs on, 14
    Earth-like worlds, 150-151
    hit by asteroids, 142
    magnetic field, 40
    North and South Poles, 40
    plants on, 94
    rain forests on, 95
    temperatures, 109
earthquake
    how to be prepared, 32-33
    earthquake-proof buildings, 33
    Earth's crust, 32
    in Chile, 33
    in Haiti, 33
    in Kobe, Japan, 33
eco-friendly house
    awnings, 175
    compact fluorescent bulbs, 175
    Energy Star label on appliances, 175
    fans, 175
    insulation, 175
    power strip, 175
    slow-flow faucets, 175
    solar panels in, 175
    tips to make, 174-175
Egypt, 68, 78
electric car
    charging stations, 101
    vs. hybrid, 101
electricity
    during storms, 28, 30
    generated by solar panels, 173
    generated by wind turbines, 176-177
    in a lightning bolt, 31
    in cars, 100-101
    in maglev trains, 105
    in microwaves, 111
    saving, 175

electromagnetic field
    in Earth, 40
    in Jupiter, 145
    in train guideways, 105
elephants
    communication in, 6
    emotions in, 6, 159
    low-frequency calls, 7
    sense of smell, 6
    social life, 6
    trunks, 6
e-mail, 120-121
Eminem, 171
emotions
    in animals, 159
endangered species, 15
energy
    Energy Star label, 175
    in microwave ovens, 110
    produced by wind, 176-177
    saving in a home, 174-175
entomologist, 19
environment
    ways to help, 174
esophagus, 156
exercise
    to help eyesight, 162
    to keep healthy, 165
    heartbeat after, 169
exoplanets
    discovered, 151
    Earth-like life in, 150
    Goldilock region, 150
eyeglasses, 162-163
eyes (animal)
    cones, 16
    iris, 16
    nocturnal, 16-17
    pupil, 16
    rods, 16
    tapetum, 16
eyes (human)
    chemicals to fight germs, 164
    cornea, 162-163
    exam, 162
    eyeglasses, 162-163
    lens, 163
    parts of, 163
    protection against sun, 149
    retina, 162-163
    tears in eyeball, 159

F

farsightedness, 163
feces, 157
Federal Emergency Management
    Agency (FEMA), 42
fire
    Fire Prevention Week, 34
    first volunteer fire company, 34
    how to stay safe, 34-35
    leading cause of, 34

firefighters
Dalmatians as firehouse watchdogs, 35
gear, 35
GPS devices, 35
helmets, 35
temperature-sensing camera, 35
fireworks
as first rockets, 154
display on July Fourth, 91
firing panel, 91
mortars in, 90-91
parts of, 90-91
pyrotechnicians, 90
shows, 89-90
fish
affected by oil spills, 84
emotions in, 159
in the Arctic, 25
poisonous, 13
and sharks, 8-9
flounder, 11
Ford, Henry, 171
fossils
finding, 80
plaster casts, 81
removing, 80-81
Franklin, Benjamin, 34, 162
Friends Disaster Service, 42
Fujikyu Highland Promenade Rink, 54

G

Galliard Cut, 72
Galveston, TX, 28
GameCube, 123
garbage, 178-179
Gates, Bill, 171
Gatun Lake, 72
Gatun locks, 72
Gayetty, Joseph, 114
generator
in hybrid cars, 100
in refrigerator, 118
in wind turbines, 177
George Washington Bridge, 75
Georgetown, IL, 95
Germany, 104, 108
germs
how body fights, 164-165
in vaccines, 160
Giza, 68, 78
glacier, 92-93
global cooling, 14
Goddard, Robert, 154
gold
as mineral, 97
in cell phones, 173
recycling, 172
Golden Gate Bridge, 75
goldenrod crab spider, 11
gorillas, 159
Gotthard Base Tunnel, 102-103
Greenland, 92-93
Groening, Matt, 171

growlers, 92
Guadarrama Tunnel, 103
guide animals
capuchin monkeys, 39
cats and dogs, 39
miniature horses, 39
Gulf of Mexico, 82-83

H

H-4 Hercules, 109
hacker, 120
hard drive, 120-121
Harrington, Sir John, 114
Hawk, Tony, 50
Hayden Sphere, 153
hearing
how loud music hurts, 166-167
heart
heartbeat, 168-169
location in your chest, 169
valves in, 168
helium
in Jupiter, 145
in the sun, 148
hiking
tips not to get lost, 41
hive, 20-21
honey, 20-21
honeybees
drones, 20
fungus and virus, 21
parts of hive, 20-21
pollen, 20-21
population, 21
queen, 20
workers, 21
Hoover Dam, 74-75
Horse Hollow Wind Energy Center, 177
Houdini, Henry, 113
Houston, TX, 146
Hungary, 76
hurricane
deadliest hurricane in U.S. history, 28
eye, 29
how to be prepared, 28-29
in Gulf of Mexico, 28
season, 29
wind speeds in, 28
hybrid car
batteries in, 100
parts of, 100-101
shape of, 101
vs. electric, 101
hydrochloric acid, 156-157
hydrogen
in the sun, 148
liquid, 154

I

ice cream
favorite flavors, 134
freezing, 135
how to make, 140-141
in history, 134, 140

ingredients in, 134
pasteurizing, 134
ice hockey
equipment, 48-49
masks, 49
rink, 60-61
rubber pucks, 48
skating speeds, 48
ice skating
axis of skater, 54
dizziness, 55
spinning speed, 54-55
iceberg
bergy bits, 92
growlers, 92
how it is formed, 92-93
shapes of, 93
immune system
ways to keep healthy, 165
India, 14, 69, 114
Indiana, 129
Indonesia, 132
insulin, 161
Interior Seaway, 14
International Space Station (ISS), 114, 146
Internet
safe surfing in, 121
Iowa, 177
Ivory Coast, 132

J

Japan, 33, 46, 54, 87, 103, 105, 108
Japan Origami Airplane Association, 108
Jeter, Derek, 46
Jollie, Angelina, 171
JP-Maglev, 105
Jumbo Tron, 61
Juno probe
putting together, 144
solar panels in, 144
Jupiter
atmosphere in, 144-145
bands and belts in, 145
facts on, 145
magnetic field in, 145

K

Keeler, Wee Willie
Keller, Helen, 171
Kelowna, Canada, 77
key
in a lock, 112-113
used by Houdini, 113
kinetic energy
in balls, 64
in roller coasters, 86
Kingda Ka, 87
Kutcher, Steven

L

lacrimal sac, 159
landfill
how to make, 178
layers of soil and trash, 179

Lee, Cliff, 171
left-handers
    list of famous, 171
lens
    in animal eyes, 16
    in camera, 125
    in human eyes, 162-163
    in periscopes, 127
lightning
    bolt, 31
    electric field, 31
    electricity in, 30-31
    how to stay safe during, 30-31
limestone, 68-69
Limon Bay, 72
liquid hydrogen, 154
Little Leaguers, 67
lock
    history of, 112
    in Panama Canal, 72-73
    parts of, 112-113
    pin and tumbler, 112-113
    Yale, 113
Lombardi's pizzeria, 138
Longoria, Evan, 46
Los Angeles Clippers, 61
Los Angeles Kings, 60
Los Angeles, CA, 123
Lotschberg Base Tunnel, 103
Louisville Slugger Museum & Factory, 67
Louvre Museum, 78
Luxembourg, 135
lymphocytes
    antibodies in, 165
    killer, 165
Lyndon B. Johnson Space Center, 146
lysozyme, 158

M

Mackinac Bridge, 75
maglev train
    current in coils, 105
    electromagnetic field, 105
    guideway, 104
    how it works, 104-105
    J-P Maglev, 105
    Shanghai Transrapid, 105
    Shinkansen MLX01, 105
    speeds of, 104
    TR-07, 105
magnetron, 111
Major League Baseball, 66
Manson, IL, 142
marine animals
    blubber in, 24
    cleaned after oil spills, 84
Mars, 150
Martin Marietta X-24, 109
McCain, John, 171
medicines
    antibiotics, 160
    insulin, 161
    time-release drugs, 161
    types of, 160-161

vaccines, 160
melanin, 10
Mercury, 150
metals
    hydrochloric acid, 157
    recycling, 172
Mexico, 69, 128
mice, 25
microwave oven
    energy in, 110
    how it cooks food, 110-111
    magnetron in, 111
    parts of, 110
    Spencer, Percy, 111
Mike O'Callahan-Pat Tillman
        Memorial Bridge
    arches in, 74
    Hoover Dam, 75
    how it was built, 74-75
    temporary cables, 74
milk
    in chocolate, 133
    in ice cream, 134-135
    in yogurt, 139
Milky Way, 152
Millennium Force, 87
minerals
    aluminum, 97
    gold, 97
    Mohs scale list, 97
miniature horses, 39
Minnesota, 177
Miraflores Lake, 73
mirror
    in periscopes, 126
modem, 123
Modica, Italy, 131
Mohs, Friederich, 97
mold, 160
monitor lizard, 17
Montreal Canadiens, 49
mortars, 90-91
motion capture technology,
    3-D animation, 62
    cameras, 62
    to help athletes, 62-63
    video-game rendering, 63
Mount Rushmore
    Black Hills, 70
    dimension of faces, 70
    presidents portrayed, 70
    tools used in construction, 71
mucus
    in stomach, 156
    in nose, 165
music
    high volume in, 166

N

NASA Near Earth Collision Program, 142
NASA, 108, 117, 144
Nash, Rick, 63
National Emergency Response, 42
NBA, 60, 61, 63

nearsightedness, 163
Nebraska, 129
Neutral Buoyancy Laboratory, 146
Nevada, 74
New York City, 91, 123, 138, 153
Newton, Sir Isaac
    third law of motion, 106
    left-handed, 171
New Zealand, 135
Nile River, 68
Nintendo, 123
North America, 15, 22
nose, 159
nuclear fusion, 148

O

Oasis of the Sea, 107
Obama, Barack, 171
oil burning, 83
oil spills,
    effect on birds, 83
    how they are cleaned, 82-83
    in Gulf of Mexico, 82-85
    industries affected by, 83
    tools to clean, 82-83
Okanagan University, 77
okapi, 27
onomatopoeia, 116
optical illusions
    afterimage, 88
    brain activity in, 89
    color contrast, 89
    complementary colors, 88
orb web, 18
origami, 108
owl, 17
oxygen
    in eyes, 162
    in rain forests, 95
    liquid, 154

P

Pacific Ocean, 73
paleontologists, 80
Panama Canal
    Gaillard Cut, 72
    Gatun Lake, 72
    Gatus locks, 72
    how a lock works, 73
    how it was built, 73
    Limon Bay, 72
    Miraflores Lake, 73
    Miraflores locks, 73
    parts of, 72-73
    Pedro Miguel lock, 73
Panama, 72
Panamanian tortoise beetle, 11
paper
    airplane, 108-109
    fibers in, 180
    how to make recycled, 180-181
    in history, 180
Paris, France, 78
Paul, Chris, 63

Pedro Miguel locks, 73
Pedroia, Dustin, 63
peppers
    heat of, 137
    Scoville untis, 137
    types of, 136-137
periscope
    how to make a, 126-127
    in submarines, 98
    mirrors in, 126
pharaohs, 68
pit viper, 17
pizza
    how to make, 138
    in history, 138
    toppings, 138
planetarium
    first modern, 152
    how to build, 152-153
planets
    Jupiter, 144-145
    Mars, 151
    Mercury, 150
    orbiting stars, 150
    seen in planetariums, 152
    Venus, 150
Plante, Jacques, 49
plants
    burdock, 117
    fossils of, 80
    how they breathe, 95
    in rain forests, 95
    life-saving, 95
plaster, 81
PlayStation Move, 123
poison arrow frog, 13
polar bear
    blubber in, 24
    layers of hair, 25
poop, 114, 157
popcorn
    how it pops, 128-129
    in history, 128
    in Native American legend, 128
    parts of, 128-129
Poppen, Sherman, 52
propeller
    in boats, 106
    in submarines, 98
pupil
    in animals, 16
    in humans, 162-163
pyramids
    Brihadeeswara Temple, 69
    Egyptian, 68-69
    how they were built, 68-69
    limestone, 68-69
    Pyramid of the Sun, 69
    ramps, 69
    sides of, 78
    to build a spaghetti bridge, 76
    tools to build, 68-69
pyrotechnicians, 90

Q
quinine, 95

R
rain forest
    fossilized, 95
    how to make, 94-95
    life-saving plants in, 95
    native plants to, 95
Reagan, Ronald, 171
recycling
    computer parts, 173
    electronic waste, 172-173
    in construction, 174
    metals, 172
    paper, 180-181
refrigerator
    compressor in, 118
    how it keeps food cold, 118-119
    invention of, 118
    parts of, 118-119
    refrigerant in, 118
retina
    in animals, 16
    in humans, 162-163
rivers,
    Colorado, 74
    Nile, 68
rocket
    how to launch, 154-155
    in history, 154
    Robert Goddard, 154
    speed of, 155
roller coasters
    centrifugal force in, 87
    kinetic energy, 86
    loop-de-loop, 87
    motorized chains in, 86
    safety bars and seat belts, 86
router, 122-123
Ruth, Babe, 67, 171

S
Sahara Desert, 29
saliva, 164
salt
    crystals, 96
    in tears, 158
Scoville units, 137
Scoville, Wilbur, 137
search and rescue (SAR) dogs
    types of, 38-39
Seikan Tunnel, 103
server, 123
Shanghai Transrapid, 105
sharks
    attacks, 9
    electro-receptors in, 9
    great white, 8
    hair cells in, 9
    lifespan, 9
    sense of smell, 8
Shinkansen MLX01, 105

Simpson, Bart, 171
skateboarding
    invention of, 50
    Tony Hawk, 50
skateboarding tricks
    hippie jump, 50
    ollie, 50-51
    pivot, 50
    wheelies, 50
skin
    as germ protector, 164
    in chameleons, 10-11
    in polar bears, 25
    in sharks, 8
    protecting against sun, 149
    sensors in human, 136
Smithsonian Institution's Air and
    Space Museum, 109
snakes
    fangs in, 12
    tips to avoid being bitten, 13
    types of venomous, 12
    venom gland, 12
snake milker, 13
snowboarding
    artwork on boards, 52
    how to do the trick called butter, 52-53
    invention of, 52
snowflakes, 92
solar system
    exoplanets, 150
    Jupiter in, 144-145
    planets in our, 150
sorbents, 82
sound decibels, 166-167
Soundback, Gideon, 116
South America, 72, 94, 128, 132
South Dakota, 70
spacecraft
    around space rocks, 143
    Juno, 144-145
Spencer, Percy, 111
spider
    how it makes an orb web, 18-19
    silk, 19
    spinneret, 18-19
Spider-Man, 19
sports
    injuries, 58-59
    motion capture technology and, 62-64
    percentage of boys and girls, 59
sports video games, 62
STAPLES center, 60-61
Steel Dragon 2000, 87
stethoscope
    diaphragm in, 168
    how to make a, 168-169
    sound waves in, 168
stickers, 83
Stingley, Norman H., 65
stomach
    acid to kill bacteria, 164
    chyme, 157
    hydrochloric acid, 156-157

lining, 156-157
   parts of, 156-157
stonefish, 13
submarines
   as weapons of war, 98
   parts of, 98-99
   USS *Nautilus*, 99
sugar
   crystals, 96
   in bread, 131
   in chocolate, 133
   in ice cream, 134
sun
   helium in, 148
   hydrogen in, 148
   in history, 148
   nuclear fusion, 148
   parts of, 148-149
   Pyramid of the, 69
   safety, 149
   sunscreen, 149
   temperature of, 148
   UV rays, 149
Super Ball, 64-65
   the largest, 65
Super Bowl, 64
supercells, 37
surfing
   big-wave surfers, 56
   Polynesian surfers, 56
   staying upright on a board, 56-57
   wave tube, 56
survival kit
   components of a three-day kit, 43
Switzerland, 102

T

Tacoma Narrows Bridge, 75
tarsier, 16
tear gland, 159
tears
   gland, 159
   how they are produced, 158
   lacrimal sac, 159
   lysozyme in, 158
   tear glands in animals, 159
temperature
   in a cosmic cloud, 119
   in Antarctica, 119
   in the Arctic, 119
Teotihuacanos, 69
termites, 23
Terrafugia Transition, 101
territory
   how cats and dogs mark, 27
   how to mark, 26-27
Texas, 177
TGV, 105
Time Warner Cable Arena, 61
Tinkham, Guy, 119
Titanic, 92
Toda, Takuo, 108
toilet
   composting, 115

dual flush, 115
   in history, 114
   invention of flush, 114
   names for, 115
   paper, 114
   parts of, 114-115
   the most expensive, 114
   water-saving, 115
Top 5
   fastest trains, 105
   favorite ice cream flavors, 140
   highest roller coasters in the world, 87
   ice cream consuming countries, 135
   longest railroad tunnels, 103
   pizza toppings, 139
   sports kids play, 59
   strangest airplanes, 109
   Wi-Fi friendly U.S. cities, 123
   wind–power-producing states, 177
Top Thrill Dragon, 87
tornado
   how it is formed, 37
   how to be prepared for, 36-37
   speed of, 36
   supercells, 37
   vortex, 37
Tornado Alley, 36
Tower of Terror II, 87
TR-07, 105
Tretiak, Vladislav, 49
Trojan horse, 120
Tunguska, Russia, 143
tunnel boring machine (TBM), 102-103
tunnel
   Channel England-France, 103
   Gotthard Base, 102-103
   Guadarrama, 103
   how it is built, 102-103
   Lotschberg Base, 103
   Seikan, 103
   tunnel boring machine (TBM), 102
TV
   radio signals in, 123
   recycling, 172
   waves, 110
20,000 Leagues Under the Sea, 99

U

United States
   cars in, 100
   ice cream consuming in, 135
   maglev trains in, 104
   poisonous snakes in, 12
   tornadoes in, 36
USS *Nautilus*, 99
Utah, 80

V

vaccine, 160-161
vanilla
   in ice cream, 134, 140
Velcro
   invention of, 117
   uses of, 117

venom
   in snakes, 12-13
Venus, 150
Verne, Jules, 99
Verrazano-Narrows Bridge, 75
viruses,
   computer, 120-121
   in body, 164
viscosity, 65
volcanic eruptions, 14
voles, 25
Vought V-173, 109
VZ-9AV Avrocar, 109

W

Washington (state), 177
weightlessness, 146
Wham-O, 65
white blood cells
   lymphocytes, 165
   macrophages, 165
Wi-Fi
   how it works, 122-123
   in cafes and restaurants, 123
   outdoors, 123
Wii, 123
wind farms, 176
wind turbines
   casing, 176
   drive shaft, 176
   generator, 176
   how they make electricity, 176
   parts of, 176-177
wind
   in hurricanes, 28
   in Jupiter, 145
   in tornadoes, 28-29
   turbines, 176-177
wireless video games, 123
Wolf, Fred, 119
World War I and II, 98

X-Y-Z

Xbox 360, 123
Yale lock, 113
Yale, Linus Sr, and Jr., 113
yeast
   active, 138
   cells, 130
   in bread, 130
yogurt
   bacteria in, 141
   how to make, 141
Yucatan, 14
zero gravity, 146-147
zipper
   in history, 116
   invention of modern, 116
   parts of, 116-117
   uses of, 117
   Velcro, 117
Zveno Bomber Fighter, 109

Credits

All illustrations and diagrams by Felipe Galindo unless indicated otherwise.
All photos clockwise from top left, unless indicated otherwise.
Key: (S) = Shutterstock; b = background image

Cover: b: Guilu (S), Kirsty Pargeter (S)
Back cover: Arto Hakola (S); Felipe Galindo; Greg da Silva (S); Quayside (S); b: Jose Antonio Perez (S)
p 1: b: Guilu (S)
p 2: Vitaly Titov & Maria Sidelnikova (S); Catmando (S); Joy Fera (S); b: Zhanna Ocheret (S)
p 3: Felipe Galindo (2); Peter Weber (S); b: Zhanna Ocheret (S)
p 4: Tim the Finn (S); Blacqbook (S); Bevan Goldswain (S); Felipe Galindo; b: Zhanna Ocheret (S)
p 5: b: slowfish
pp 6-7: Villiers Steyn (S); Blue Ice (S); Whale: Brandelet (S)
pp 8-9: Nastya Pirieva (S); Roger De Marfa (S)
pp 10-11: agoxa (S); Jacek Jasinski (S); CLChang (S); Henrik Larsson (S); Bark: slowfish (S); b: Shebeko (S)
pp 12-13: Both snake illustrations by Dorling Kindersley/Getty Images; Sidebar: Chris Hill (S); Stephan Kerkhofs (S); Pete Niesen (S); Snake: joroma (S); b: Pan Xunbin (S)
pp 14-15: Bierchen (S); Andrejs Pidjass (S); Vishnevskiy Vasily (S); Triff (S); Sidebar: Jason Prince (S); b: Catmando (S)
pp 16-17: Vitaly Titov & Maria Sidelnikova (S); Ammit (S); Hugh Lansdown (S); Ilya D. Gridnev (S); EcoPrint (S); b: hinnamsaisuy (S)
pp 18-19: Spider: Arto Hakola (S); Photo of Steven Kutcher by Harry Chamberlain, courtesy of Steven Kutcher, http://home.earthlink.net/~skutcher/; b: Anyka (S)
pp 20-21: Beehive illustration by Lon Tweeten and Ed Gabel for Time; LilKar (S); Apple and orange: Nattika (S); Cherries: Serg64 (S); Bee: Dani Vincek (S); b: LilKar (S)
pp 22-23: Dam by Pete Ryan/Getty Images; Illustration by De Agostini/Getty Images; Bowerbird: Janelle Lugge (S); Caddisfly: Picavet (S); Termite nest: EcoPrint (S); b: Thomas Barrat (S)
pp 24-25: Tony Campbell (S); JG Photo (S); jaytee (S); b: Uryadnikov Sergey (S)
pp 26-27: Joy Brown (S); Art_man (S); Hung Chung Chih (S); b: Khoroshunova Olga (S)
pp 28-29: Notebooks by vovan (S); Hurricane illustration by Joe Zeff Design, Inc. for TIME For Kids; b: Kirschner (S)
pp 30-31: Clipped papers by Robbi (S); Fesus Robert (S); b: Martin Fischer (S)
pp 32-33: Notebooks by jomphong (S); arindambanerjee (S); Yai (S); b: Njegovic (S)
pp 34-35: Clipped papers by Robbi (S); AnetaPics (S); nodff (S); Mishella (S); Kovalchuk Oleksandr (S); b: Rechitan Sorin (S)
pp 36-37: Notebook by nuttakit (S); Ryan McGinnis/Getty Images; Illustration by Eric Nguyen/Corbis; b: R. Gino Santa Maria (S)
pp 38-39: Thinkstock/Getty Images; AFP/Getty Images; AFP/Getty Images; Jim Frazee(S); Jim Parkin (S); Miniature horse photo by Neil Soderstrom from Panda: A Guide Horse for Ann by Rosanna Hansen (Boyds Mills Press); b: Tatagatta (S)
pp 40-41: Golden Pixels LLC (S); Elinag (S); b: Febris (S)
pp 42-43: Lisa F. Young (S); Christopher Elwell (S); Mazzzur (S); Gregory Gerber (S); American Red Cross photo by Doug Pensinger/Getty Images; b: Lisa F. Young (S)
pp 44-45: steamroller_blues (S); Gears illustration by Felipe Galindo; b: Andrey Yurlov (S)
pp 46-47: All photos by Al Tielemans/Sports Illustrated; b: Monkey Business Images (S)
pp 48-49: Bruce Bennett/Getty Images; Lebedinski Vladislav (S); Olivia Barr (S); Jacques Plante

photo by Time & Life Pictures/Getty Images; Vladislav Tretiak photo by Robert Riger/Getty Images; William Melton (S); b: Losevsky Pavel (S)
pp 50-51: Robert Cianflone/Getty Images; b: Baronb (S)
pp 52-53: Snowboards by Alex Ciopata (S); b: Ipatov (S)
pp 54-55: Olga Besnard (S); AFP/Getty Images; b: Maxim Tupikov (S)
pp 56-57: Mana Photo (S); b: Gustavo Miguel Fernandes (S)
pp 58-59: Peter Weber (S); R. Gino Santa Maria (S); Tomasz Trojanowski (S); Matthew Leete/Getty Images; FIFA via Getty Images; b: muzsy (S)
pp 60-61: All photos by John W. McDonough
pp 62-63: All photos courtesy of Donna Moxley Scarborough, MS, PT & Eric M. Berkson, MD of the MGH Sports Performance Center, Department of Orthopaedics, Massachusetts General Hospital
pp 64-65: b: bezmaski (S)
pp 66-67: Coprid (S); Louisville Slugger Museum & Factory photo © Hillerich & Bradsby Co.; b: Richard Paul Kane (S)
pp 68-69: Brian Maudsley (S); Victor V. Hoguns Zhugin (S); Marcos Carvalho (S); Raj Krish (S); Pius Lee (S); b: R-O-M-A (S)
pp 70-71: Jody Dingle (S); All historic photos courtesy of National Park Service, U.S. Department of the Interior
pp 72-73: Stan Shebs/Creative Commons; Thomas Marine, Library of Congress; b: B. Franklin (S)
pp 74-75: Bridge under construction and inset photo by Nigel Photography; Finished bridge by Jamey Stillings; Illustration by Stephen Blue for TIME For Kids; Sidebar photo by Jumper/Getty Images
pp 76-77: Factoid photos by Wayne Moore, Castanet News; b: Jeff Banke (S)
pp 78-79: Factoid photo by tungtopgun (S); b: R-O-M-A (S)
pp 80-81: Photos 1, 2 and 3 by Curtis Slepian; David McNew/Getty Images; b: Louie Psihoyos/Getty Images
pp 82-83: Joe Raedle/Getty Images; Chris Graythen/Getty Images; Cheryl Casey (S); Sidebar photo by Joe Raedle/Getty Images; b: Danny E Hooks (S)
pp 84-85: AFP/Getty Images; Justin Sullivan/Getty Images; David McNew/Getty Images; Photos 1 and 2 by AFP/Getty Images; b: Spencer Platt/Getty Images
pp 86-87: Margie Hurwich (S); Sylvie Bouchard (S); Rachel Grazias (S); Joy Fera (S); Stacie Stauff Smith Photography (S); Sidebar photos: Kingda Ka: Dusso Janladde/Creative Commons; Millennium Force: Coasterman1234/Creative Commons; Tower of Terror II: Creative Commons; b: mahout (S)
pp 88-89: b: privilege (S)
pp 90-91: Spencer Platt/Getty Images; Young Yun/Getty Images; Altrendo Travel/Getty Images; New York Daily News/Getty Images; photo #3 by Guy Calaf/Polaris; b: Steve Kelley/Getty Images
pp 92-93: Steve Estvanik (S); jele (S); Vince Reichardt/Getty Images; Pete Ryan/Getty Images; b: Jan Martin Will (S)
pp 94-95: Ricardo Esplana Babor (S); Dmitriy Kovtun (S); b: Wong Yu Liang (S)
pp 96-97: Diamond, salt and sugar crystal photos by Creative Commons; Talc by Manamana (S); Calcite by Jiri Slama (S); Quartz by optimarc (S); b: Mirka Moksha (S)
pp 98-99: Factoid photo by SuperStock/Getty Images; b: Sergey Orlov (S)
pp 100-101: Bill Pugliano/Getty Images; Terrafugia (x3); AFP/Getty Images; b: Jordan Tan (S)
pp 102-103: evan66 (S); Handout/Getty Images; b: evan66 (S)
pp 104-105: Maglev photos courtesy of Transrapid USA; J-P Maglev by Creative Commons; Shanghai Maglev photo by Lee Prince (S); b: mamahoohooba (S)
pp 106-107: Creative Commons; b: Tool Using Animal (S)
pp 108-109: Public domain; NASA (x2); b: Vera Volkova (S)
pp 110-111: Creative Commons; Vadym Andrushchenko (S); b: Natali Glado (S)
pp 112-113: Popperfoto/Getty Images; b: Adisa (S)
pp 114-115: Einar Muoni (S); Hadrian (S); b: Ryoh (S)
pp 116-117: Zipper illustration by Scott Weichert/Getty Images; Torsten Dietrich (S); Keetten Predators (S); b: Caro Sheridan/Splityarn/Getty Images

pp 118-119: Volodymyr Goinyk (S); Gentoo Multimedia Ltd. (S); NASA; b: wonderisland (S)
pp 120-121: R studio T; Elnur (S); Balefire (S); Rischgitz/Getty Images; Todd Davidson/Getty Images; Computer by Shortkut (S); Sidebar background by Zhanna Ocheret (S); b: Bofotolux (S)
pp 122-123: From left to right: Greg da Silva (S); Norman Chan (x2); Jules Frazier/Getty Images; Map by R studio T; Sidebar photo by AFP/Getty Images; b: Zhanna Ocheret (S)
pp 124-125: SSPL via Getty Images; Murat Baysan (S); b: Moreno Soppelsa (S)
pp 126-127: Matt Ragen (S); DEA/L. Pedicini/Getty Images; b: Andrea Danti (S)
pp 128-129: Kernels by Bevan Goldswain (S); b: Roxana Bashyrova (S)
pp 130-131: Steve Gschmeissner/SPL/Getty Images; Ian O'Leary/Getty Images; Steve Baccon/Getty Images; Mark Thomas/Getty Images; Peter Dazeley/Getty Images; b: Roman Gorielov (S)
pp 132-133: Photo 1: Norman Chan (S); 2: N. Frey Photography, Maceofoto (S); 3: Creative Commons/GNU, Maks M (S); 4: Frederic Prochasson (S); 5: kentoh (S), pulsar75 (S); 6: Creative Commons/GNU; b: ARENA Creative (S)
pp 134-135: All photos courtesy of Turkey Hill Dairy; Sidebar photo: ifong (S); b: ifong (S)
pp 136-137: John Whitley-Gibson; Privilege (S); Stephen Mc-Sweeny (S); Quayside (S); Marc C. Johnson (S); b: IKGM (S)
pp 138-139: Joe Gough (S); Roxana Bashyrova (S); Lasse Kristensen (S); b: Olga Nayashkova (S)
pp 140-141: b: M. Unal Ozmen
pp 142-143: Explosion photo by Adastra/Getty Images; Rocks by Tim the Finn (S); b: Creative Commons/GNU
pp 144-145: All photos by NASA except solar system by Stocktrek Images/Getty Images
pp 146-147: All photos by NASA; b: Mack7777 (S)
pp 148-149: All photos by iStockphoto.com
pp 150-151: Planet photo illustration by iStockphoto.com
pp 152-153: Factoid photos by Creative Commons/GNU; b: Ken Freeman (S)
pp 154-155: b: Jose Antonio Perez (S)
pp 156-157: new wave (S); 3D Clinic/Getty Images; Roger Harris/SPL/Getty Images; b: Creations (S)
pp 158-159: Life Boat/Getty Images; pokku (S)
pp 160-161: voylodyon (S); StillFx (S); simurg (S); Dmitry Lobanov (S); Blend Images/Ariel Skelley/Getty Images; Sebastian Kaulitzki (S); b: Sebastian Kaulitzki (S)
pp 162-163: Diagrams by Dorling Kindersley/Getty Images; After David Martin/Getty Images; b: Bomshtein (S)
pp 164-165: Gleb Semenjuk (S); Purestock/Getty Images; Coneyl Jay/Getty Images; National Cancer Institute; Sebastian Kaulitzki (S); Blacqbook (S); Hand photo by Shkurd (S); b: argus (S)
pp 166-167: Oguz Aral (S); dwphotos (S); b: Zwola Fasola (S)
pp 168-169: b: Sashkin (S)
pp 170-171: Michel Setboun/Getty Images; Alex Wong/Getty Images; David McNew/AFP/Getty Images; Mark Rucker/Transcendental Graphics/Getty Images; b: Dhoxax (S)
pp 172-173: Jyrki Komulainen/Getty Images; Sean Gallup/Getty Images; AFP/Getty Images; Sport Moments; Sean Gallup/Getty Images; b: rezachka (S)
pp 174-175: b: Vera Volkova (S)
pp 176-177: TSpider (S); Map by R studio T; b: majeczka (S)
pp 178-179: b: rezachka (S)
pp 180-181: b: alexkar08 (S)
pp 182-191: b: Zhanna Ocheret (S)
pp 92: b: Guilu (S)